ROB ANTHONY

THE $1,000,000

WEB

A PRACTICAL GUIDE
FOR WEALTH AND
FREEDOM AS AN
ONLINE FREELANCER

DESIGNER

GUIDE

Contents

Note from the Author

Every day I get several emails like this...

"I am sick of my job and want to quit so I can start building my own business…"

"I just finished university and haven't been able to get a real job. I feel I didn't learn anything..."

"I feel depressed and want to start making some real progress in life…"

"I wish I could travel more with my girlfriend, but I don't have the savings or the ability to take time off..."

"I want to help support my family but my new business idea is going nowhere…"

"I feel like if something doesn't change, soon I will have to give up and get a job…"

If you can relate, this book is for you.

Hi, I'm Rob O'Rourke, founder of Fox Web School. Maybe you found me through YouTube or one of the other places I post online. Either way, I wrote this book to help you succeed with web design and business in general. I want to see you win—and win big!

This is a no BS guide to selling profitable website projects. I am going to share with you specific tools and tactics that I learned to become a successful web design freelancer earning over $100,000 a year during my first year in business. This is the best information I picked up from my own journey and from helping several thousand other web designers succeed.

Also, this book isn't just about web design. While I love web design, it should just be one step on a journey to bigger success. This book is really about you and how you can make yourself into the best business owner and entrepreneur you can be. I want to give you a clear roadmap that you can begin using today, so this book contains practical advice and steps you can take starting right now.

If you are ready to find out what I wish I had known when I first started web design (and entrepreneurship) several years ago, then let's get going! This book is designed to be read in a few hours but to have a lasting impact over the next few years of your business journey.

INTRO-
DUCTION

A Tale of Two Web Designers

Question: Why do some web designer freelancers achieve great success while others fail?

Meet Dave

Dave was about to call it quits. The past year had been extremely challenging for him, both financially and mentally. He was left feeling frustrated and confused by his lack of success as a freelance web designer. After all, Dave was fantastic at designing websites. Everyone told him so.

During his university years, all of his professors were impressed by his technical expertise and his innovative design skills. After graduation, he went on to work as a front-end developer for a highly-respected software company. As part of a large team, he was in charge of focusing on UX design and branding.

It was a job many people would love to have—a full-time, decent-paying role with great benefits, paid vacation, and office-catered lunches.

But after only two years, Dave was already experiencing the dreaded burnout. Before starting this job, Dave had heard that tech companies were notorious for their fast-paced working environments, but he did not realize just *how* fast-paced the company culture would be.

Even though he worked diligently during the day, he still had to put in extra hours to finish every project. He often came into the office early and left late at night, sometimes working 12+ hour days. And it wasn't just him putting in overtime—he noticed that most of his co-workers worked crazy hours and nearly everyone seemed exhausted, even many of his superiors.

Feeling that this burnout had no end in sight left Dave feeling conflicted and unhappy. He knew that he needed to improve his current situation, but wasn't sure how. One thing he knew for sure is that he hated working so many extra hours. This was not only because it meant that he had less time to spend with his girlfriend and his loved ones, but also because his overtime work did *not* equate to more money in his pocket.

His initial thought was that he should ask for a raise. He figured more money could at least make up for the extra hours. Dave requested a performance review with his supervisor. He went in prepared to ask for a 15% pay increase, but he was bombarded with reasons why he did not deserve such a "big" raise. After more negotiation, he settled for what was offered—a mere 5% increase over what he was already making.

After doing some quick math, Dave felt even *more* hopeless. He realized that to see a real change in his quality of life, it would take a significantly larger raise or years of saving. And even if he received a significant raise one day, he would still be forced to put in unlimited overtime hours to no benefit of his own. His extra hours would only benefit the company, which would grow more profitable thanks to his hard work.

He realized he was working to fulfill someone else's dream instead of his own. The writing was on the wall, but he had ignored it for so long. Dave finally realized that, as an employee, it does not matter how hard you work—the results are always going to be the same.

At this point, Dave knew that he needed a better option. He wanted to do something that would allow him to take control of his life and set his hours instead of being a slave to his busy schedule. He also wanted to prioritize the relationships that meant the most to him.

Dave and his girlfriend, Ana, always talked about giving up all of their belongings and moving to the mountains. They both loved nature and being active. Dave had always dreamed of taking up snowboarding, while Ana wanted to learn to ski, and they both wanted to get away from the hustle and bustle of city life.

Dave decided it was finally time to find a way to make this dream a reality. He wanted the ability to work anywhere and set his sights on becoming a web design freelancer. He already had the skills and expertise, so he thought working for himself would be easy.

His only initial concern was money. Even though he held a decent-paying job for over two years, he had failed to add much to his savings account and was living paycheck to paycheck.

After having a lengthy discussion with Ana about his desire to work for himself, Dave decided he would quit his job. He wanted to give one hundred percent of his attention to becoming a successful freelancer, so they could make their dream life a reality sooner. Ana would keep her full-time job for the time being to help support them both in the beginning.

Feeling confident about his decision, he put in his two-week notice the following week. He had no doubt he would succeed in his new endeavor. With his background and impressive design portfolio, he was sure any business would jump at the chance to work with him.

Fast forward to the first anniversary of Dave quitting his job. In the past year, Dave had only signed on five small clients, even though he made endless cold calls and sent hundreds of emails, gave dozens of proposals, and had taken multiple additional online web design and coding courses. While hearing "no" when offering his services was discouraging, the lack of responses to his efforts discouraged him the most.

To make matters worse, he was making far less than what he made with the software company. While some months were better than others, Ana was covering the majority of their rent and bills.

This financial burden was starting to put a significant strain on their relationship. Dave could tell that Ana constantly worried about money, and he felt helpless to do anything about it. He had tried everything to make his business successful, but felt like a failure. The worst part for him was that he hadn't just let himself down, he let Ana down too.

Dave knew that he couldn't keep freelancing like this for much longer. If he did, he would be broke, single, and further away from his dream than before he quit his job.

Feeling desperate and out of options, Dave opened his inbox. With a slight hesitation, he pulled up the email address of his former manager to see if his old company was hiring.

Meet Ricky

In the same city, only a few blocks south of Dave, Ricky had a completely different experience with his freelance web design business.

In stark comparison to Dave, Ricky was in awe of the success of his business. While the first few months of freelancing were slow, it wasn't long before he started experiencing exceptional growth.

In just over a year, he had gained multiple new web design clients through both referrals and cold-calling. Now, he was consistently selling website redesign projects between $5,000 and $15,000 and had built up over $8,000 in recurring monthly revenue.

With all of this success, it can be hard to believe that it had only been just over a year and a half since Ricky left his old 9 to 5 job to pursue freelancing full-time.

In fact, before starting his web design business, Ricky had no web design experience at all.

Growing up, Ricky had always liked doing things his way, and from the time he was in high school, he already knew that he would never be happy living the same cookie-cutter lifestyle that many of his friends wanted. He had no desire to own a large house in the suburbs and didn't care about driving a luxury car. He wasn't interested in owning things—he craved experiences—and he dreamed of escaping the rat race altogether.

But Ricky's family put a lot of pressure on him to go to university so that he could graduate and get a "good" job. He was naturally inquisitive, but shy, so he decided to study to become an engineer.

During his school years, Ricky was lucky enough to meet a girl who later became his wife. As his graduation date inched closer, he again thought of his desire to escape the rat race. He and his wife began dreaming of moving to a place that was warm, beautiful, and more connected to nature. After hearing a friend's experiences in Bali, and how there was a large expat community on the island, the couple decided to set their sights on moving there.

Together, Ricky and his wife decided that after graduation, they would both get full-time jobs until they were able to save enough money to afford to pay off debt and make the move.

Within a few months of graduating, Ricky was offered an electrical engineering role for a corporate telecommunications company—the exact type of job he had always dreaded. However, it paid well and would allow him to save a lot of money, so he accepted the offer.

While he hated the stuffy and bureaucratic work environment, he did find joy in using his engineering skills to solve problems. He had always loved learning about how things worked and finding ways to make them work better.

Even though Ricky excelled at his job, he quickly tired of all of the corporate bureaucracy. He knew that he would not keep this job forever, but it still felt difficult to make it through the workday. After less than a year, Ricky began to feel depressed and unfulfilled.

Nevertheless, he tried to stay positive. He knew that his wife, Heather, did not love her job either, and he tried to always keep their Bali dreams in the back of his mind.

Then, one day, Ricky came across a surprising opportunity.

"Ricky, I really want a new phone. Mine is so old. It doesn't even have two cameras, let alone three," said his wife's youngest sister, Erin, during one of her monthly visits to his house.

Ricky couldn't help but laugh and roll his eyes.

"Right, Erin, a new phone like that costs at least $1,000 and you are still in high school. What do you even need a new phone for anyway?"

"You already know I like to draw a lot but I didn't tell you yet—I started a little project a while back. I have been drawing a lot of portraits of my friends and posting them on Instagram. Quite a few people have started sharing them and the page has started to take off. You should see the number of followers I have racked up in just the last few months," said Erin.

She showed Ricky the page. It had over 5,000 followers and was growing by a few hundred each day. Each photo had hundreds of likes and dozens of comments. He was impressed.

"What has started happening recently though is that people are DMing me all the time to ask how much I would charge to turn their photos into drawings. Last week, one girl even offered to pay me $200! I think, with better photos I could sell a lot more."

"That's a great idea. You probably could sell even more if you also had a place to list your prices, and maybe even a way for people to submit their photos automatically and pay you online," said Ricky.

"Yeah, a website. I know. But I don't know how to make one."

"I'll make you one," said Ricky, surprising himself.

"You know how to do that?!"

"Not yet. But I will learn."

This conversation would prove to be a defining moment in his career. It was the first website of many that he would design. And it was the last time Ricky would do it for free.

Flash forward a year and a half from that very first website, and Ricky had come a long way. What had started as a fun side project to help his wife's little sister had grown into a full-blown business.

As Ricky's business had grown, he had focused on implementing systems that would allow him to work less, while shifting his focus to doing what he enjoyed: closing big sales and communicating with clients.

He enjoyed what he did, but he also wanted to build the business in a way that it could eventually run itself. Plus, he saw what burnout looked like for others at his engineering job, and he had always thought it would be best to avoid this if he ever ran his own business.

With this in mind, Ricky turned his focus to fast growth and implemented smart systems, which allowed him to achieve a decent work-life balance after his first 18 months of business.

Then, he expanded his services to offer SEO, ads, and copywriting and was able to hire a small team to help with about 80% of the actual client work. With the team in place, Ricky would usually only work roughly three to four hours in the morning and have the rest of the day to do as he pleased.

With less responsibility and most of his new web design sales coming in through referrals and warm leads, Ricky had more time to learn about other things that interested him. He found himself drawn to health and fitness—he began exercising twice daily and even learned to cook a variety of healthy meals from scratch.

The more he cooked, the more he found himself engrossed in learning about nutrition and food. He had recently built a website for a new food delivery company and he was surprised to see that most of their customers were very motivated by healthy living, not just convenient and tasty treats. After some research, he learned that there was a growing local trend of people who grew their own food and that there were even more people who wanted to start but didn't know how.

This research got Ricky thinking: *What if there was a place nearby for people to learn about growing their own produce, without having to own land?*

Seeing a potential need, Ricky began searching for plots of land just outside of his city. He was surprised to see that there was an abundance of plots and older farms near the coast that were available for cheap.

He began to put together a business plan and shared it with Heather. She loved the idea—so much that they decided to put their Bali dreams on hold for a little longer.

Over the next few months, Ricky and Heather created a detailed vision for their new business: a trendy eco-farm and hostel where visitors can learn all about growing their own food and enjoy activities like surfing, yoga, and cooking classes. Although they wanted something profitable, they also wanted to create a business that offered real value and made a difference. They even planned to use some of the business profits to invest in communities that didn't have access to fresh food.

Ricky knew that a few businesses like his eco-farm already existed, but he also knew he could quickly gain the top spot with his newfound skills in web design and marketing. Even though it was a bit of a gamble, he knew he could make it work. Ricky saw there was a massive opportunity to build a better website than his competitors, rank it properly on Google, and run effective ads. He felt confident that if he had the best marketing plan, it would get him the customer numbers and cash flow to build the best possible eco-farm.

Over the next year, Ricky and Heather put their plan into action and watched it unfold. Although it started small and wasn't an overnight success, it quickly began to snowball, thanks in part to a great marketing plan. Each new group of customers loved their experience, which resulted in a lot of positive reviews and shares online.

Eventually, they were able to hire a full team, including local farmers and hostel staff. They recruited a friend to manage the hostel full-time. This allowed Ricky and Heather to handle marketing and bookings, which they eventually managed from their villa in Bali.

In just three years, Ricky had achieved both financial independence and his dream of moving to Bali—all without working a traditional 9 to 5 job. And he had no plans to work for someone else ever again.

A SIMPLE QUESTION

Why do some web designers, like Ricky, achieve great success while others, like Dave, fail?

The question seems simple on the surface. Unfortunately, the answer is not as simple as it may seem. Traditional thinking would tell us that Dave should have been successful, since he had the professional background and skills that we are all taught that we need to succeed.

Ricky, on the other hand, did not have a web design background. He did not know any advanced coding languages and had never worked for a highly-respected tech company.

Yet, he succeeded in quitting his job, starting two successful businesses, and achieving financial independence after only a few years.

Why?

Because Ricky learned something that few web designers ever learn—coding and design techniques come second to solving problems and providing value. And with this knowledge, he figured out how to escape the rat race and was able to create a life of freedom and wealth.

This book will show you how *you* can be successful, just like Ricky.

Freelancing is a Step in the Right Direction

Before we move further into this book, here's another question to consider:

Why do you want to become a web design freelancer?

In my experience, I've found that most people start freelancing because they want more control over how they live their lives.

Some people, like Dave, dream of escaping to the mountains. Others, like Ricky, want to escape the rat race and pursue their interests, while also giving back to the community. For you, it may be the desire to have complete financial security and freedom, the ability to spend more time with your children or spouse, more time to focus on your true passions, or the desire to change the world.

Whatever the reason, you probably have been told that being an employee is not the way to take control of your life and achieve your dreams. On the surface, this makes a lot of sense—when you work for someone else, you get a steady paycheck, but you lose most of the freedom (and profits) you can enjoy while working for yourself.

This loss of freedom is why many aspiring web designers initially turn to freelancing. Freelancing is indeed a great place to start.

Freelancers have the chance to learn a lot of valuable skills, such as client communication, time management, design, and technical skills. Freelancers also gain real-world experience and can begin to understand how business works while adapting the mindsets and habits needed to succeed in life and business.

If you want to become a business owner, it's essential to view freelancing as a temporary stage in your professional career.

Why?

Because even if you end up as the highest-paid freelancer around, you are still going to eventually limit yourself from hitting your bigger business and life goals. The freelancing model, while great to start with, can quickly hold you back from even greater success.

If, instead, you only use freelancing as a temporary stage on your path to success, you can win. The trick is in knowing exactly what freelancing traps to avoid and how to plan ahead.

This book will show you how.

So how do you play the freelancing game to win?

One thing you need to know right from the start is that you do not want to get stuck in freelancing forever.

As a freelancer, you are still someone who trades time for money. You may feel like your own boss, but in many ways, you are just a slightly more independent employee, a contractor.

The challenge as a freelance web designer is **you** are the business. If there is work to do, it's up to you to complete it. If you need more clients, you must be the one to make the sales. And if there are mistakes, it's up to you to fix them.

Freelancing is great at the start—you do all the work and get all the profits. But the better you sell, and the more work you get, the quicker you will reach your limits. Your success can crush you.

If you miss a day, you don't get paid. If you take a month off, then your business does too.

After a few years (or less) of this, you will realize that freelancing does not make you *free*. Again, this doesn't mean freelancing isn't suitable to start with—just that you need to start planning for the future right now.

So what is a better goal than just freelancing forever?

Become a real business owner as soon as possible.

The difference: a business owner *manages* a business, while the freelancer *is* the business.

A business owner can enjoy growing their business as much as they want—they have the systems and team to do so. But the freelancer is stuck in the middle—they often end up working 60- to 80-hour weeks as their "own boss." The more they make, the less freedom they actually have.

How can you avoid the freelancing-forever trap?

Learn to think like a business owner from the very start.

You still begin with freelancing, but your focus is much different. Instead of freelancing with only the next paycheck in mind, you carefully plan how to use every opportunity to transition to being a business owner as soon as possible.

Think of your freelancing time as a paid education in becoming a real business owner.

Using the right web design freelancing approach (which we will cover in this book), you can quickly make this transition to a business owner. The next few chapters will cover how to build the skills, the knowledge, the mindset, and the cash flow to make the jump.

This way, you can freelance short-term while still creating massive long-term potential for yourself.

To show this in action, I want to share with you the journey of MJ DeMarco, author of *The Millionaire Fastlane* and creator of the Fastlane Forum.

MJ never really set out to be a web designer, but he knew that he wanted to build massive wealth and live life how he pleased. If you know his story, you know he did just that. His story effectively illustrates how one can go from an underpaid employee to a temporary freelancer to a successful business owner.

In just seven years, MJ went from living at home with his mother as a broke 26-year-old to becoming a multimillionaire by age 33. So how did he do it?

While his path to success wasn't easy or straightforward, his burning desire for a better life led him to find a way to make it happen.

Let's start with MJ at age 26. He is working a dead-end job as a limo driver to pay his bills in his home city of Chicago. His goal is to quit, move someplace sunny, and get rich. Sounds fun (of course!), but he has one problem—he sees no real way to make any of that happen.

One day, though, while plotting his escape, one of his wealthy limo riders happened to ask him if he knew of a reliable limo service in New York City. MJ did not know the answer, but it got him thinking: if this was a problem for one frequent traveler, it must be an issue for many others (keep in mind this was pre-Uber and no such online car booking services yet existed).

Seeing a huge opportunity to create an online limo booking business, MJ quickly got to work on building the skills and cash flow needed to make it happen. He realized to make this business a reality he would first need to be able to build a website. Before this, he knew nothing about creating websites, so he quickly started learning the basics of web design and marketing.

Then, something unexpected happened. As MJ worked on getting his idea off the ground, other businesses saw the potential for MJ to help them too. They could see he was having increasing success in marketing his own business online, and they wanted to pay him for his growing expertise.

In his book, MJ DeMarco writes:

> Then one day I had a breakthrough; I received a call from a company in Kansas who raved about my website service and wanted me to design their website. Sure. I obliged with a price of $400. They thought the price was a steal and within 24 hours, I built the company their website. I was ecstatic. In 24 hours, I had most of the rent payment.
>
> Then ironically, not 24 hours later, I received another call from a company in New York asking for the same thing… a new website. I designed theirs for $600 and it took me two days to complete. I had another rent payment! Now, I know this isn't a lot of money, but from poverty to $1000 in three days felt like winning the fifty-million-dollar Powerball.

This interest resulted in MJ starting a temporary side business creating websites. While his web design business paid his bills and improved his coding skills, it was also allowing him to master the other skills like marketing, building systems, and sales that he would need to turn his big business idea into a massive success.

By combining a great opportunity with a temporary web design freelancing gig, he was able to improve his skills and savings. MJ was then able to turn his big idea from just a thought into a big real-world success while netting him several million dollars along the way.

Did he continue doing web design forever? Of course not. But he used that opportunity in the best way possible and combined it with the skills and the right mindset (which we will cover in this book). And MJ isn't the only one. A look at many top online and offline entrepreneurs will show a background in web design, coding, or other similar skills. The reason? Web design is one of the best niches for anyone who wants to get moving towards their big goal, while also picking up the skills they need along the way. That is as long as you *approach* web design freelancing it in the right way, of course.

[Note: I highly recommend checking out the **Fastlane Forum** and MJ's book The Millionaire Fastlane. I post under the username Fox on the forum, and you can tag me in your posts to let me know if you join].

◆◆◆

The Success Logic

The road to success is not always straightforward. Most people stumble along the way and take a few (or *more* than a few) wrong turns before finding the right path.

But the road to success does not have to be so messy. By looking at my own journey (which I will share with you later) and the journeys of other successful people, I have found logical steps you can take to streamline your path to success.

Now, I am not saying this will make finding success easy—you will still face rejection and failure along the way. But this will ensure that you are staying on the success path and not wandering off into the forest.

Here is the first part of the 3-Step Success Logic:

❶ **The best way to reach long-term success is as a business owner.**

There is a common trend with the successful people that I have met, studied, or personally known—they were able to create an amazing life through owning and managing a successful business. Why? Because business owners get rewarded for the value their business creates. They build something that can operate and generate profit *without* them being physically present.

This means they often only have to work when they want to. If the business owner decides not to work, then the business still operates as it usually would. This option to not work allows them to make money when they sleep, go on holiday for a month, or work on other ideas and projects. When Elon Musk takes a week off work, Tesla or SpaceX don't need to shut down!

Business owners also use the power of scale. One barber can only cut so many heads of hair in a month because they are limited by their personal time and energy. But someone who creates a barber franchise or a range of shampoos can sell as many shampoos as they want. They build the business in a way that allows it to grow readily, without requiring them to do more personally once the business is up and running.

As an employee, freelancer, or sub-contractor, though, this isn't the case. You don't get to enjoy endless time off or watch your business grow rapidly overnight. You only get paid for your ongoing work.

Working as an employee or a freelancer also means that, no matter how talented you are, the moment you stop working is also the moment you stop earning more money. It is an endless cycle of work -> get paid -> start more work -> get paid -> do more work.

This cycle means that, as an employee or a freelancer, if you want to earn more, you will also have to do more. If you go on holiday or buy a new car, then that money is directly linked to you working more hours. And since your time and energy are always going to be limited, it becomes a very stressful and draining way to support your long-term goals and plans.

So, while freelancing can be a great place to start, at its core, it is a system that limits you severely in the long-term. The bigger your end goals, the more you will have to work to fund them, and the less time you will have to enjoy what you are building. You can't win long-term with this approach.

The better approach? *Only* use freelancing as a temporary stage, where you can learn and prepare to become a business owner. Just like MJ Demarco, you should focus instead on using freelancing to gather the skills, resources, and opportunities needed to move to the next level. You still make money right now, but you also create a solid foundation that allows you to move to the next level of true freedom.

Logic #1   Your end goal should be to become a successful business owner. Becoming a business owner allows you to succeed in life without requiring never-ending amounts of your personal time or energy.

❷ **The way to become a successful business owner is by first learning to solve problems and provide value.**

Many people think, *If I just had the money, I could start a successful business now.* But that is only true for someone who already knows how to play the game of business. Without the proper business mindset and experience, a person with a lot of money is still likely to fail. It isn't that they do not want to succeed; it is that they simply are not yet ready.

A good analogy is that making money and running a successful business is a lot like flying a plane. It is possible to fly a plane safely and successfully, but only once you know how to do it. If you just hope that it will work, without any training or skills, then it is very likely you are going to crash. Giving someone who isn't ready a profitable business to manage is a lot like giving a fighter jet to someone who just watched *Top Gun*. It just isn't a good idea.

A successful business owner, just like a good pilot, has a solid foundation of training, experience, and confidence. It isn't luck or a big loan from the bank that keeps them winning—it's their foundation of real skills and experience. It is *because* of previous failures and learning experiences that they now know what they are doing, and they can calculate what a smart choice is and what approach has the best possible chance of success. They win because they prepare to win.

For you to be ready to become a successful business owner, you, too, need to start working on building the necessary skills, experience, and confidence.

You will need to be able to spot a great opportunity and also have the ability to make it possible. If you do not prepare, then you will just be playing a game of luck, just hoping you win. Since you are reading this book, though, I know that isn't you, so let's look at a great place for you to get started.

Logic #2　The way to become a successful business owner is by first learning to solve problems and provide value. To succeed as a business owner, you need real skills, training, and experience.

❸ One of the best places to learn the bigger business skills needed to succeed is through first learning to run a profitable web design business.

Now, this might seem like a big leap, but let me share what I have learned.

I have studied hundreds of different niches, and very few tick as many "business-owner skills" boxes as web design. Quite simply, web design is possibly the best place to start learning the skills you need to succeed in business.

I could write an entire book on the business skills web design can teach you, but, instead, I'll name a few that really stand out: prospecting, sales, pricing, cold calling, cold emailing, networking, client communication, project management, copywriting, marketing, building sales systems, ads, email marketing, managing a team, managing yourself, and many others. That's *a lot* of skills.

Because of the unique way in which web design requires you to both run your own business and directly help other businesses you will learn a lot in a short amount of time. As long as you focus on the right areas and clients (covered in this book), every new project is an opportunity to learn directly from an experienced business owner while solving new problems and challenges.

At its core, when it is done the right way, web design is creative business problem solving at work, which means that a few months of web design freelancing can give you valuable business experience and skills that can take you years to obtain elsewhere.

Also, it is very easy to get started in web design with little or no resources. You don't need a $90,000 student loan or the "right" insider connections. Nor do you need $50,000 to invest in stocks or merchandise. All you need is the ability to take action and an internet connection. As long as you have those, you can start to learn the basics of web design. It has zero risks and plenty of upside potential.

There are a lot of other reasons why running a web design business is a great starting point, but I won't list them all here, but I will cover more of them as this book moves along.

For now, let me emphasize that web design is a great choice for preparing for your bigger future plans right now. If this aligns with your goals, then read on. The rest of this book will show you what you need to know to get started right away.

Logic #3   If you are looking for a place to get started building real business skills, then consider looking at how the right approach to web design can make this possible.

◆◆◆

WHY SHOULD YOU READ THIS BOOK?

While there are a lot of web design books and courses on the market, this book is different from what you will find with other resources.

This book does not focus on UX design, programming languages, or web server management. It won't teach you the basics of HTML and CSS or how to create a responsive website.

This is not because you shouldn't learn these things—just that these skills are secondary to your success. Remember, your end goal should not be to become a long-term web designer but to use web design to become a successful business owner.

The main goal of this book is, instead, to help you think differently, and then (and only then) show you how to take action. You can learn code almost anywhere—this book is about developing the skills and mindset needed to think like a business owner.

This book will also show you that there is a competitive advantage in the web design game—and it is not superior design skills—and you can take advantage of it. If you use what I will show you, you will see it is possible to make both rapid progress and some great profits in a short amount of time.

As you read this book, you will follow along with the stories of Dave and Ricky to illustrate the difference between a successful and a struggling web design freelancer. This book will show you why someone like Ricky was successful, and why Dave's approach left him in a worse place than where he started. Every day, web designers are either acting like Ricky or like Dave. My purpose with this book is to make sure that you stay on the right path to victory.

My intention when I wrote this book was to make it fun, informative, and straightforward. There are no "get-rich-quick" gimmicks in these pages—only real-world advice that will steer you in the right direction, so you can take control of your career, finances, and life. It is a resource that I wish I would have had available when I first started.

The main goal of this book is to help you succeed. Along with the advice in this book, check out the additional resources in Chapter 12 for other useful resources to get started. These extra resources are useful as you advance through this book.

If, after reading this book, you would like more personalized help to accelerate your business success, you can opt to work with me through my ongoing group-coaching program, Fox Sales Legends. This program has resulted in a lot of student success stories and helped put hundreds on the right path towards financial freedom. You can find more details about the Fox Sales Legends program here: **https://foxwebschool.com /foxsaleslegends/**

Meet the Coach

Hi, I'm Rob O'Rourke, but a lot of people call me Fox. The name Fox is a bit random, as it was the username I picked when I first started posting online, but it stuck.

In 2016, I started Fox Web School, and have since enjoyed directly coaching hundreds of students and helping thousands of others through various courses and training resources. I also make educational YouTube videos and post often on the Fastlane Forums.

I wasn't always a coach, though. In fact, I am naturally very introverted, and not a big fan of the "coaching space" in general. But seeing others make progress and succeed has motivated me to ignore my natural introverted ways and build the best web design business school I was able to. It is a big personal challenge, but I love every day of it.

For me, coaching happened by accident: in 2016, I started posting online about my progress as a new web designer and shared what was working for me. Soon, I had a lot of people reaching out to ask for help, so they too could find similar success.

I was happy to help, but I quickly became overwhelmed. At one point, I was getting 50+ personal emails and messages per day and figured there had to be a better way to pass on what I had learned. This is how Fox Web School started.

While I now often get asked for business advice and feedback, I would like to point out that before web design and the school, I, myself, experienced a lot of failures. Looking back now, I can see these failures were where I learned so much. Unfortunately, failure is also where I see so many others give up and quit.

To show you how many failures it can sometimes take to succeed, let me run through a brief history of what I did before starting web design:

- My business ventures began with a string of crazy childhood business ideas that made little money and often got me into trouble.
- At age 17, I moved from Ireland to New Zealand, where I quickly went broke and ended up working as "the head of maintenance" in Burger

King. My job consisted of cleaning the ice cream machine daily and stacking hundreds of trays of burger buns.

- Upon returning to Ireland, I picked a random degree to escape to university.
- I somehow managed to graduate with a degree in Construction Engineering right before Ireland's largest construction recession ever. The degree is now worthless.
- With zero real job offers, I got a job working in a sports camp playing with kids on a water trampoline. I got to surf a lot, but I couldn't see a future for an entrepreneur in the trampoline industry.
- It took me over a year to save enough to get plane tickets to Edmonton, Canada, where a friend had told me there were oil jobs.
- Upon arrival in Canada, I had only a few hundred dollars left and had to sleep on a bench my first night because I missed my airport bus transfer.
- After months with dozens of different manual labor jobs, usually outside in blizzard conditions, I eventually ended up with a decent, well-paying oil job.
- Success! But it only lasted a year before a massive oil recession hit. No more oil job.
- With no other jobs lined up and since I had saved very little, I got on a plane to Colombia, where another friend informed me that the cost of living was super cheap.
- While in Colombia, I set the goal of making enough money to stay there permanently.
- Teaching English seemed like a good idea. I quit/got fired almost immediately.
- Next, I started an Instagram book review page, and after a month of work, I only managed to get around 30 followers. I didn't even know how it was supposed to make money, so I moved on.
- Around this time, I paid a developer to make an app that auto messaged other people on dating apps. My crazy idea was to enable people to "auto message" thousands of people at once. It never took off, but the developer did steal the code, anyway, to sell online.

- Next, I made a Conor McGregor cereal box with my buddy. Selling $1 cereal for $25 seemed like a smart idea until we got shut down by Conor's management team. (If you want to check some of these schemes out, search "Conor McGregor Cereal Box" or "Turbo Talk for Tinder" online. Ha!)

After all of this time, the only good idea I had was a Spanish school booking website.

While living in Colombia, I looked for a Spanish course but found the process of finding a school and paying online was a total nightmare. I threw together a very basic website that listed a few schools and managed to make a few thousand dollars in commission.

This idea had a lot of potential, but I did not have the skills needed to grow it at the time. I figured it might be a good idea to learn more about making websites and see what happens.

If you think some of the ideas I listed above are ridiculous, you are 100% right. I wanted you to see this list of failures to show you that learning to succeed in business can take time and that you should not let past failures hold you back. When I first started, I would often blame other people and make excuses for my failures, but now I see my approach and mindset at the time were all wrong.

I'd like to say that by the time I started my web design business, I had things all figured out, but that wasn't the case either. I still had a lot to learn. My first months were spent building websites for $100 to $200 on Upwork, with no idea of how to make more money.

After building yet another standard website for a low-paying client, it finally hit me—I am making nothing because these websites are *worth* nothing. It wasn't about how hard I worked—it was about how much value I created (or did not create)—and this was a very important business lesson for me.

I realized that if I wanted to change how much I was getting paid, then I needed to provide more than some just fancy website design. I realized businesses were only going to pay me real money when I was able to show them real results. I needed to produce big results if I wanted a big paycheck!

With this new approach and mindset, the business quickly took off.

The very next website I did sold for $2,000 because it focused on helping the business get a lot more sales by solving their online booking problems. At the time, this was more money than the months of other smaller projects combined!

Next, I helped an engineering company with a website that could land them large new projects and got paid $7,000. It was huge money for me, but a great deal for them.

Within the next six months, I was getting paid up to $20,000 per website because I was able to show how they solved real-world problems, provided a ton of value, and significantly helped my clients.

On paper, increasing your prices from $100 to $20,000 in one year like I did might seem crazy. But with the right approach, *you* can do it. This book can show you how to do it, too, and how to get started right away.

Ready? Let's get right into it…

◆◆◆

HOW TO BEST USE THIS BOOK

This book is broken down into three distinct sections.

Chapters 1–4 are the *Mindset* chapters. The information in these chapters is absolutely essential. It is necessary to *really* take your time as you read these pages to make sure you fully understand the material before moving on to the next section.

Chapters 5–8 are the *Action* chapters. Here, we still scratch the surface of the steps you need to take to become a successful freelance web designer and beyond. It is necessary to read these chapters only if you have made it through the Mindset section.

In the last section, Chapters 9–11, you will find Parting Advice and Wisdom.

In the last chapter, Chapter 12, you will find additional resources available to you through Fox Web School.

Also, I want you to check out the link below for a series of emails that go with this book. We want to see you succeed, and these emails are written specifically to keep you on track and moving forward. After helping 1,000s of other people succeed, we will give you our top pieces of advice and action steps.

To sign up for these free emails, just go here: **https://foxwebschool.com /extrahelp**

I hope you are excited to start this journey and dip your toes into a new way of thinking. With that being said, let's jump into the Mindset chapters.

SHIFTING YOUR MINDSET

CHAPTER 1
SELL A RESULT, NOT A WEBSITE

A website is just the tool.

Welcome to the first *Mindset* chapter.

I know you are eager to get your web design freelance business started or to turn your existing web design business into a success. If you are like most people dedicated to achieving a goal, you are probably looking for actionable advice that will drive you in the right direction.

But before you take action, you must first consider your mindset.

I want to tell you something now that will save you many headaches down the road:

Adopting the right mindset is absolutely *essential* to your success.

As I mentioned in my personal story above, I had many unsuccessful business ventures before starting one that was profitable. I attribute my failures to not having the right mindset, and I want to help you avoid making the same mistakes that I did.

The next four chapters will help illustrate the importance of adopting a new way of thinking.

For now, let's check back in with our two web designers.

Dave's Lost Opportunity

Dave walked out of the air-conditioned office and slammed the door.

"That guy doesn't know a thing about web design," he muttered under his breath. "A complete website redesign for under $3,000 is a total steal. Whatever. It's his loss."

The website redesign Dave had proposed was nothing short of amazing. It was custom-built, hand-coded, would load in under 0.5 seconds, and Jack, Dave's UX designer friend, would design a beautiful interface.

Dave was introduced to Pete Thompson through an old university buddy. Pete owned a large renovations business in the city and was facing an increasingly competitive market. He had a great team that could transform any property, but they were having a tough time landing new customers.

People just didn't know that much about Pete's business, and they would often choose to work with one of his well-known competitors instead. If Pete did not turn things around quickly, he would need to lay off some of his staff.

When Pete confided about his troubles to an old friend, his friend suggested that he should show more about what makes his business great online to help attract suitable clients. This idea seemed logical, but Pete knew nothing about websites or promoting a business online.

He asked around, and his nephew recommended a web designer named Dave. With a meeting scheduled, Pete was feeling optimistic.

Dave was also feeling optimistic—he had put many hours into his proposal, and he could hardly wait to present it. On the day of the meeting, Dave practically skipped into Pete's office and was greeted by his secretary. After a few minutes, Pete welcomed Dave into his office.

"It's great to meet you, Dave. My nephew had a lot of great things to say about you, and I really appreciate you taking the time to come in today. If I'm being frank, business has been tough lately. I really need—"

"Don't worry Mr. Thompson. I know just what your website needs," said Dave, beaming as he pulled up his proposal deck on his laptop.

"Oh. I was not expecting a presentation today. I was just thinking we could talk a bit about my current business circumstances," said Pete. "And please, call me Pete."

"Mr. Thompson, I pride myself on being an experienced, professional web designer. I know you are going to like what you see."

After 30 minutes of explaining the ins and outs of his designs, Dave finished his proposal. He knew Pete was impressed. In fact, he was speechless—he had not said a word the entire time.

Finally, Pete spoke.

"Okay… Dave, this all looks very impressive. But I'm on the verge of having to lay off some of my staff, and $3,000 is a big investment. How is this new website supposed to help me get more business?"

"Uhh…." stammered Dave, and then found himself unable to answer the question. The passing seconds felt like hours.

Pete stood up and offered his hand. "Thank you for your time Dave, but I do not think we are going to be a good fit. I really appreciate you coming out."

Dave grunted as he shook Mr. Thompson's hand.

◆◆◆

A Valuable Lesson

If Dave had paid attention, he would have learned a valuable lesson that day. This lesson is so valuable it can change everything for a new web design freelancer, so I want to make sure to share this lesson with you.

Are you ready?

Here it is:

You are not selling websites. You are selling results.

Let me repeat that: *You are selling results. To a business owner,* the results your website can get them is all that matters.

I know this may sound confusing at first. Web designers, whether formally educated or self-taught, are told to sell websites by focusing on design, code, and fancy features. But while these things can make a website look good, they are not what will get you high paying jobs or happy clients.

When pitching your services to business owners, you must remember that results are what sell. In short, the more problems you can solve, and the more results you can show, the easier it is to get high-paying web design work.

Think of it like this: For a business owner, a website is only ever a tool.

It is just one possible option amongst many that they can choose to invest in to improve or grow their business. The business owner could instead hire new staff, buy more equipment, invest in their factory, buy a new company car, buy advertising space, and more. When selling websites, you don't compete against other web designers—you compete against all the business owner's other options to get the desired end-result for their business!

Now that might sound like really tough competition, but it isn't. When you know how to focus on exactly what a business owner needs and how to get it for them, you will quickly stand out.

Most other web designers miss this. They focus on their price or how many pages they can build or the advanced features they can design. They miss the big picture, and the business owner doesn't buy it. Instead, you should always be thinking: *What results does the business owner desire? What are they really looking to get when they spend their money?*

To be successful with web design, you need to stop thinking in terms of code, design, and fonts, and instead, see how these elements can be used in a meaningful way to help a business advance towards its goals. The design should look good, but what makes it sellable is that it actually achieves something. You need to sell what end-result the website can achieve.

The great thing is that this doesn't require advanced coding skills—you do not need to be a brilliant designer or an expert coder. You can get started right away with very minimal technical skills as long as you understand that people pay for results, not websites.

While Dave missed out on this lesson, Ricky was lucky enough to spot it. It was this approach and not his technical skills that got him working with Pete Thompson on a $3,000 web design project just a few days after Dave's failed pitch. But more on that in a moment.

◆◆◆

Ricky's Mindset Shift

Ricky was out for an after-work happy hour with his coworkers.

As he took a sip of his drink, he overheard his coworker's friend talking about a problem.

"My uncle really needs something to turn his business around. He said he desperately needs some new clients. His friend put him onto the idea of updating his website, so I recommended my web designer friend, Dave, but man, did he bomb the meeting! I'm not sure what he's going to do next."

Ricky sat up straight. *This could be my chance*, he thought.

"Hey, April, who's that guy over there? He's your friend, right?" Ricky probed his coworker. "Could you introduce us?"

It took some convincing, but after a conversation, Ricky was able to get a recommendation from Pete's nephew. Now with a meeting set, Ricky had a lot of work to do.

After several hours of watching YouTube videos on modern web design trends, Ricky had come up with a proposal of his own. Since he had only just finished his first website a few weeks prior, he asked his wife if she would act as his audience. His confidence was shaky at best.

Nervously, Ricky started presenting his proposal. His voice shook as he spoke, and he stumbled over his words.

After a few minutes of suffering through this awkward presentation, his wife stopped him. Gently, she began to speak.

"Ricky, I know you've put a lot of hard work into this project, and I have so much respect for you for doing so. But right now, you do not sound confident about how this can help Pete Thompson's business. All I am hearing so far is how you think you can make his website *look* better."

Ricky took a second to collect his thoughts.

"You're right—I guess I *don't* feel confident at all. To be honest, I feel like a total imposter. A few weeks ago, before I helped your sister, I knew nothing about web design, and here I am talking about a bunch of random design features like I know what they are. I just don't see what I can say to get this guy to want to buy a website. It just doesn't seem right."

"Ricky, when you helped my sister with her photography idea you had a clear goal in mind—you wanted to help her show off her work and allow people to pay online, yes?"

"Yeah…"

"Ricky, this is the same. This business owner is not going to pay you for the latest design trends. He wants to know what you can do for his business," his wife said. "When you spoke to the owner's nephew, he was speaking of problems his uncle was facing in his business. What were those problems?"

"Hmm, he said that his uncle needed new clients. And if he didn't get them soon, there would be layoffs," answered Ricky.

"So, how can you use a website to help him get more clients?"

Ricky did not know the answer yet, but his wife's question did shift his way of thinking.

View Websites as Tools of the Trade

As we've started to see in this chapter, results are what sells, not websites. Before we move on to the next chapter, I want to give you one last example to help make this idea stick.

Imagine you go to the dentist tomorrow with a terrible toothache. Every day for the last week, this tooth has been causing you excruciating pain, and you have found it difficult to focus on anything else.

When you tell the dentist about your toothache woes, will you be thinking about what brand of drill he is going to use, or what type of chair you will sit in during the appointment?

No! Of course not.

At that moment, all you care about is finding relief to your pain and getting your teeth back to normal. As long as you can trust the dentist to make you feel better, you aren't concerned about how he is going to make that happen, because all you want is for the pain to stop.

It is the exact *same* situation for a business with a problem.

Every business has issues, challenges, and pain points. These are the tooth-aches. When you are trying to sell a website to a business owner, you need to show clearly how it can solve a problem or make the pain go away. If you don't clearly show what a website can do for them, then they will not see any compelling reason to pay you to help them. It would be like a dentist showing you a cool new drill during the appointment instead of actually using it to make your pain go away.

To get businesses to pay you, you must always connect your website pitch to their biggest pain points. If all you do is talk about code or design aspects, the business owner won't be able to make the connection to how *your* website can solve *their* problem, which means they are unlikely to hire you no matter how good your website may be. Instead, they continue to suffer in silence—or decide to work with someone else who can offer a clear solution.

Mindset Shift Recap

❶ Sell a result, not a website. A website is only ever a tool.

CHAPTER 2

Business Owners Always Care Most About Their Core Business Needs

Not design, coding or technical aspects.

As we move on to our next *Mindset* chapter, remember our first lesson: results sell.

When we focus on finding business problems and then getting valuable results, we are thinking in a way that makes it very easy to get high-paying clients. You see, business owners don't care all that much about the latest software or newest design ideas—they trust that they can leave that stuff up to you, the expert.

What business owners *do* care about, though, is their top business needs.

These top needs are their main problems, frustrations, and challenges. In other words, these are the things that need to change so the business can grow and improve. These are the needs that are essential to doing business and typically affect a business's bottom line. If they get fixed, the business grows. If they don't, the business suffers.

You may think that, as a web designer, you need to know every single coding language or have incredible technical expertise to compete with web design agencies that have been around for years, but that is not necessarily the case. To quickly pull ahead of the competition, you need to be a web designer who approaches building websites as a way to address the most important business needs. You show this by providing solutions and results.

Let's face it—there are already tons of free or inexpensive ways to build a website without having any knowledge of coding or good design practices, which means the skill of web design itself is just not that profitable anymore. Any kid with a laptop can set up a good-looking WordPress theme within a few minutes.

So, how do you make good money as a web designer? You focus on doing things differently by solving real problems. It isn't about the design or the code or some cool trend. To land clients who are willing to pay you more than the going rate on Fiverr, you need to be doing more to help their business than just creating a basic website.

You need to be able to help them tackle and solve their top business problems.

◆◆◆

THE NEVER-ENDING BUSINESS "TO-DO LIST"

I want you to imagine a list of **everything** a business owner might possibly want to fix about their business. Picture a never-ending business "to-do list" that lives permanently in their heads. And nearly every day, this list grows a little bit bigger.

For a typical business owner, this list can be hundreds, maybe *thousands* of items long. This list may include anything from the lack of new sales this month, to the broken lightbulb in the factory storage room, to a spelling mistake on page 14 of the website. It may also include worries of hiring or firing, paying the phone bill, too many employees taking sick days this month, whether the bins have been emptied, or the current political or economic environment.

Yikes—that's a *lot* of problems.

And if a business owner tried to fix all of these problems at once, they would quickly go crazy.

So what do they do instead? They focus first on a handful of pressing problems that they consider the most urgent or serious and ignore almost everything else.

So what about the rest of the things on the list? Well, these are mentally moved to "later," which usually means never. By the time the current most-pressing problems are taken care of, there are always new, pressing problems to deal with, which means minor problems rarely get attention. Basically, if you want to persuade a business owner to do anything, you need to make sure it addresses a top business problem.

What this means for you as a web design freelancer is that you need to focus primarily on the **top priorities** when selling your websites. If you don't make your website project a top priority in the mind of the business owner, then it quickly disappears down their mental to-do-list, never to be seen again.

You speak to top priorities by first uncovering what the top priorities are and then showing how a website can help with those areas. When you do this, a website suddenly looks to the business owner like a great way to move the business forward—rather than another random "later" item to add to the list.

Selling a website based on just design or code doesn't speak to a business owner's top priorities. Design and code may be what web designers consider to be top priorities, but they are not so in the world of business.

The problem with focusing on some low-priority item is that, while a broken link on page 5 of the website is a real business problem, it's too far down on the business owner's to-do list for them to have time or energy to care. You are talking about item #347 on their mental list, and they only want to hear how to fix items one through ten, if that.

As an example, let's consider the needs of Pete, our renovations firm owner. Pete has been in the same office for over 20 years. The air conditioning doesn't work in the break room, there is paint peeling in the corners of his office, and there is a stain on the carpet in the reception area. There are hundreds of other small things that need some of his attention.

This doesn't mean Pete doesn't care about his business. In fact, he notices these things every day, and has the best of intentions to fix them in the future. But, unfortunately, within his competitive business environment, he doesn't have the time or resources to make these things a priority. He has to focus on what matters most for his business right now. The smaller stuff just has to wait.

Knowing what we know about Pete's business, let's take a look at his business to-do-list.

#1. Get new clients

#2. Improve monthly revenue

#3. Figure out long-term plan to attract more clients

#4. Pay off some of the business' credit card balance

...

#205. Fix photocopier ink issue

#206. Update website images and text

#207. Take down Christmas lights

#208. Check in with Sammy about this year's local golf tournament

Looking at this list, it should be pretty obvious what Pete's most important business needs are. Let's start at the top of the list:

- **Priority #1:** Get new clients ASAP so that he can continue to pay all of his current employees, as well as his other business expenses. Getting new clients will buy him some time to figure out what he can do next.
- **Priority #2:** Start improving revenue consistently, so he does not have to constantly worry about his firm going out of business each month. Improving revenue is the second most important task after accomplishing priority number #1.

And where is the website?

Right now, it is way down the list at #206.

Why? Because Pete has not yet seen how a website can help him with his most important problems. He is an old-school guy (as a lot of business owners are), and, to him, a website is just a bunch of text and images. Until someone shows him otherwise, or until all his bigger business problems are gone, which is unlikely, it will always be *way* down towards the bottom of his mental list.

If you can understand this, then you can see why Dave failed to sell Pete on his website idea. Dave had the best of intentions, but while trying to sell his website, he only focused on points that were towards the bottom of Pete's to-do list. Why should Pete care about a new website design when he needs to land new clients now and work on improving his revenue? Pete just didn't see the connection between Dave's new website pitch and his big problems, so he moved on.

Ricky, on the other hand, was able to convince Pete that a website, built the right way, should be the number one priority on his to-do list. He was able to clearly show how a properly planned website could solve his most important business problem: attracting new clients.

Speaking to Pete's top business need is what got Ricky a $3,000 deal, while Dave never even got a follow-up email.

◆◆◆

A Win for Ricky

Let's go back to Ricky as he plans what exactly he should say when he first meets Pete Thompson. Ricky was still thinking about the question his wife had asked: "How could a website get Pete and his renovation business more clients?

Ricky decided to reach out to his friend, Kim, who had recently hired some contractors similar to Pete's business to fix up her house. He told her about his proposal for Pete and asked if she would give him some background on why she picked the company she did and how the renovations turned out.

After speaking with Kim, Ricky found out a few important things.

First, Kim told him that she lives in her childhood home, so because of all the memories, it's very important to her. She wanted to make sure that whomever she hired would get the job done right.

Next, he found out that she didn't know anyone who did renovations, so she began her search online. She said she looked at about ten websites for renovation companies in the area. When he asked her if she happened to come across Pete's website, she said that she did, but because it lacked information, she was unsure if he could help, and moved on to the next company.

After some more searching, Kim finally landed on one website that stood out: it featured lots of information that highlighted the company's fast and professional service, and it promised that the job would get done right the first time, with no hidden fees.

She also found pictures of past projects, stellar customer reviews, and a staff page, complete with smiling staff headshots. Kim was impressed and already felt like she would be in good hands with this company.

Their number was featured at the top of the website, so Kim decided to give them a call right away. She was delighted that a real person answered the phone and that the person was able to answer all of her questions. Kim was impressed and happy by how easy and simple the process was, so she decided to hire this company for a $50,000 renovation project.

Before hanging up, the contractor asked Kim how she heard about their business.

"I actually found your website! I was really impressed by all of the reviews and photos," she replied.

"Thank you! We're glad you found it helpful," the contractor said. "Actually, since updating our site, we've been getting about half a dozen new projects a month from people who find us online. It's been a game-changer for our business."

A few months later, Kim added her own positive review to their website. And she made sure to tell all of her friends about her great experience.

After hearing Kim's story, Ricky felt inspired. His mind was racing with ways to improve Pete's website and help him get new clients.

He pulled up Pete's current website and started taking some notes.

Here are some of the things that caught Ricky's eye:

- Confusing layout; the site is difficult to navigate
- The information on the site focuses on how Pete's business started 20 years ago but doesn't focus on the quality of their work
- There are no reviews
- The only pictures on the website are photos of Pete's workshop
- No "Team" page

- There is a "Contact Us" page, but it doesn't motivate people to call. This page also contains information on where delivery truck drivers should go, which is distracting to a potential customer

With all of these things in mind, Ricky felt ready to come up with a solution.

As he started putting together a proposal, he made sure to focus on showing Pete how he could best utilize his website to attract new customers and stand out among his competitors. While Dave focused on the website's appearance, Ricky focused on learning why people buy and then creating a website that focuses on selling.

A few days later, Ricky walked out of Pete's air-conditioned office and practically jumped for joy.

My first real client, he thought, overjoyed.

Just an hour earlier, he had been waiting nervously outside the office as he went over his plans for Pete's business and his website in his head. He had done a lot of preparation but still didn't feel very confident because it was his first-ever website sales meeting.

After a few minutes, Pete welcomed Ricky into his office.

"Hello, Mr. Thompson, it's nice to meet you. My name is Ricky," he said as she extended his hand. "I really appreciate you taking the time to see me today."

All day, Pete had felt apprehensive about meeting with another web designer, but he still did not have a solution to his problem. He had to give him a chance. After a slight hesitation, he shook his hand.

"Nice to meet you too, Ricky. Please, call me Pete."

"Yes, of course, Pete. I'm very excited to be here. Your nephew told me a little bit about your current business situation, and I want to do anything I can to help. I've done some research and have a few ideas to share, but first, I was hoping you could talk me through everything that's been going on and share any other problems you have. That way I can consider the whole picture and suggest the best solution."

Pete felt his apprehension begin to melt away. He invited Ricky to have a seat, and then he started to tell him about the business challenges he had been facing recently.

The whole time Pete spoke, Ricky listened diligently and jotted some notes in his legal pad. After speaking at length about his business situation, Ricky was surprised when Pete said he did not think that a redesigned website would be the answer to his problems.

"I'm still a little unsure as to how an expensive website is going to help me get more clients. I need to get the word out to those who have never heard of my business. I was thinking I should maybe try some outdoor billboards. I see them everywhere, so they clearly must be working."

Ricky took a second, and then he began to speak.

"Thanks for sharing, Pete. I can tell you care deeply about your employees and will do anything to keep them with the business," said Ricky. "I can completely understand your hesitation about a website being the answer to your problems."

Pete nodded.

"But the truth is, a website can be extremely valuable if you use it correctly. After all, a website is only a tool. So, if we view your website as a business tool, we need to make sure it can accomplish what it was *designed* to accomplish."

"Okay…"

"So the main issue I see: while speaking to me, it's easy for you to explain why you have such a great business, and how you can help people by performing high-quality renovations, but the problem is, I doubt you get very few chances to have these types of conversations."

"Go on," said Pete.

"From our conversation today, it seems that several years ago, people would drive by the store and call in to talk, or possibly people would hear about you through a friend or neighbor. Either way, these people would come to your shop, and they would be able to see the showroom or your factory out back. Then, you could show them in person why your business was so great, which resulted in a lot of sales."

"Yes, this is true," said Pete. "We tried building a bigger sign out front, but it is rare someone driving past wants to stop and talk anymore. And we just don't get as many word-of-mouth referrals as before, either."

"Here's what I would suggest: instead of waiting for people to stop by your shop, you need to showcase on your website why your company is so great, so more people can find you. We can use your website to feature pictures of your renovations, your team, reviews, and more. This way, people can see the amazing work you do and your affordable prices without having to step foot in the store. This means that you don't lose out on potential clients who go to your competitors before you even get a chance to talk to them personally."

Pete was impressed. Finally, he felt like someone was listening to his concerns and recommending an effective solution.

He knew this would help solve his problem, and he wanted to make it happen. He asked Ricky to name his price.

From their earlier conversation, Ricky had learned that a typical renovation client was worth between $30,000 and $50,000 or more.

"Pete, I want to do the best work I can, so my price reflects having what I need to make that possible. I am asking $3,000 for the full project," said Ricky, trying to muster up as much confidence as possible. "That is only 10% of the price of a new renovation project—and I expect that the website will help you get a lot of them."

"You've got a deal, but only if you can get started right away. I can't wait much longer!"

Ricky beamed as he shook Pete's hand.

BUSINESS NEEDS COME FIRST. EVERYTHING ELSE COMES SECOND.

As you can see, Ricky had a completely different outcome from his meeting with Pete than Dave did.

The reason for this is because Ricky spoke to his business needs, while Dave did not. He knew that the importance of design and technical aspects came second to sales and business growth.

In other words, Ricky focused on Pete's top business needs and showed how his website could address these needs. Dave focused on the needs at the bottom of his list, as he spent most of his proposal time talking about design. He was speaking the language of a designer—not that of a business owner.

Speaking of Dave, let's check back in with him a week after his failed proposal with Pete.

◆◆◆

DAVE'S ONGOING STRUGGLE

Dave could not believe it: another wasted effort.

"What am I doing wrong?" he said to no one in particular. He felt angry that he had blown his chance again.

This time, it was his sister who had connected him to a potential new client.

After chatting with her friend Angela, a local wedding and event photographer, his sister learned that her business was doing really well—in fact, maybe too well. She was getting more calls than ever and was starting to feel overwhelmed. These calls were taking up a lot of Angela's time, and most of the callers had the same questions.

"Some days it feels like my phone is ringing off the hook, and I can't catch a break," Angela shared. "Last night, I was so behind on my photo editing, that I had to stay up until midnight to get everything finished. Don't get me wrong—I'm thrilled that business is good, but I don't know if I can continue to stay on top of everything."

"Yeah, that sounds tough. What are you going to do?" asked Dave's sister.

"Well, I talked to one of my photographer friends, and she said I should add a detailed contact form to my website so people can email me all their info and questions at once, and then I can send back answers and pricing. She said it cut down on the number of phone calls she's getting. Oh, and she also recommended adding more information about how the photoshoots work, and how to schedule them, and so on, so all those questions are answered upfront. It all sounds great, but I don't have any time to mess with all that."

"Well, you are in luck, because my brother knows how to do all that stuff. Let me get you his number…"

Later that evening, Angela gave Dave a call and told him everything she had told his sister earlier. Feeling excited by the prospect of a new client, Dave got to work on his proposal.

While Dave was interested in helping Angela, he also wanted to make sure this new website showcased his skills and looked as trendy as possible. He was running out of money and needed a portfolio website that stood out to help him get new clients fast.

Earlier in the week, he had come across a local web design competition. There were award categories for various web design elements, including a category for Best Overall Website Design. He knew if he could win that award, he could add it to his portfolio website and call himself an "award-winning" web designer. That would sound very impressive!

Feeling confident, Dave mocked up an idea for a website that would really let his design skills shine. The site mock-up looked incredible, and he was sure Angela would love it.

This is why Dave was surprised by Angela's reaction when he showed her his design.

Instead of smiling or looking appreciative, Angela stared blankly.

"But where is the new detailed contact form?" asked Angela. "And what about all the information for booking photoshoots?"

"Well, a big, detailed contact form won't work well with this minimalist design style. I think it's best to just list your phone number and a select few personal details, to keep the rest of the site looking professional and slick. Instead, we can focus on showing more of your cool photos and adding bits of text slide in from the sides as you scroll down through the page. I worked on a launch for a new fashion website once, and they loved this style," responded Dave.

Angela seemed to be in disbelief. "Dave, I don't really get this plan," she said. "Even if it did work, my phone is only going to be ringing more often."

"Well, the whole idea of the website is to build a lot of mystery around your brand and make visitors curious to find out more. In fact, I've designed your website *so* well that I am thinking of entering it in this local website award competition. If the website won, it could mean a lot of shares online and may even be featured in some tech news articles. If we win, you could even link to them from the bottom of the site to show people," said Dave, excitedly.

Angela went red in the face.

"So, you're telling me that you want to remove existing information *already* on the website to focus on the new layout so... *you* can win some design award?"

"Yeah! It's great, isn't it? So, what do you say?" replied clueless Dave.

Angela said she would let him know. Unsurprisingly, he never heard back from her.

◆◆◆

START AT THE TOP OF THE LIST

In this chapter, you were introduced to the concept of a "business to-do list." This list is based on the fact that business owners always put their time and energy into their most important items first, often ignoring or forgetting other less-important tasks.

I want you to keep this image in mind every time you pitch a web design project.

Before preparing the proposal, ask yourself: *Will this address a business need at the top of the list? Or would this suggestion address a need at the bottom of the list?*

Remember, a business is always most likely to take action on their core business needs. *These* are the areas where an owner will focus their time and energy, and where the money is most likely to go. If you can position yourself as someone who can provide a solution to their most important needs through your web design project, then you will always be in demand.

Mindset Shift Recap

❶ Sell a result, not a website. A website is only ever a tool.

❷ Business owners always care most about their core business needs; not design, coding, or technical aspects.

CHAPTER 3
THE MARKET PAYS YOU FOR THE VALUE YOU CREATE

Not for your time, effort, background, or education.

As we enter into our third Mindset chapter, we have already learned that results sell and that business owners always care most about their core business needs.

With both of these things in mind, our next lesson seems logical: the market pays you for the value you create.

Ricky's story proved this.

Pete was happy to pay him $3,000 because Ricky framed his website as a way to fix Pete's major problem: not attracting enough new clients. In Pete's mind, it was worth spending thousands of dollars on Ricky's website plan because, if successful, it would help him in a much larger way by landing him new clients. In other words, he paid Ricky because he created real-world value; he didn't care if Ricky had an expensive university education, prior work experience, or technical knowledge.

Had Pete cared about such things, Dave would have been the clear winner. But he was not.

Ricky was the underdog in this scenario, but yet he came out on top because he could see what Pete needed and could create a clear plan to help him get it. He proved that you don't need to be technically amazing to solve problems and find the best solutions. All that you need is the right mindset and the ability to listen and focus on what is really important.

◆◆◆

WHAT IS VALUE?

So, what do I mean by value?

When thinking about the concept of value, you first need to understand that businesses view value (and decisions on how to spend money) differently than individuals.

As an individual consumer, you buy things for various reasons. You might go see a movie for entertainment, or buy a jacket because it's the latest style, or visit a city because you've heard it is a popular new tourist spot.

Since people no longer live in caves and hunt for food, we can spend money on things purely for fun or entertainment. We are often motivated by our desire to feel good, rather than our basic needs. Simply put, there are a lot of things we as people might find valuable—it isn't just about survival.

Businesses, though, see things differently. For them, it is often *just* about survival.

If you look at the business environment today, you will see a cut-throat world where only the top businesses survive. There are always bigger and more established companies to compete with, new competitors popping up, and new taxes and regulations every year that demand attention.

If a business fails to improve or wastes money by spending on non-essential expenses, they run a high-risk of putting their business into a bad situation.

Maybe you can think of some examples of this in real life. We usually know of someone who started a new business and worried too much about how things looked rather than worrying about making actual money.

A few months go by, and while the business looks cool, in reality, it is doing poorly because it is not generating revenue. The owner may be having fun "playing business," but there are not enough real clients or customers to sustain it. It won't be long until they run out of money, and the business fails for good.

The difference with a smart owner is that they instead focus on using their time, money, and energy on business areas that actually matter. When spending money, they will try to gauge where exactly they need to put their dollars to achieve the best results. For every transaction they make, they are looking to get the maximum business value in return.

Understanding how businesses view value is essential for you as a web design freelancer.

With this understanding of value, you can start to see that your websites must create business value. This value could mean helping a business compete, grow, or improve. If you can show how your website can help the business accomplish these things, it will be much easier for you to sell your websites.

To win as a web designer, you need to always think about what a business values most, and how your website can create that value.

How Does a Website Create Value?

As you learned earlier, a website is best viewed as a business tool. For a tool to be truly valuable, it must help a business solve its problems.

Let's look at an example. If you work in construction and you need to cut some wood in half, then the most valuable tool is something that will help you slice the wood, like a saw. Likewise, if you need to build something with timber, you now need a tool that allows you to bind the wood, like a drill or a hammer.

Just like in the construction example, the "perfect" tool changes to match the current challenge or problem you are facing. This is the same for businesses.

If a business has a problem getting enough sales, then they need a website that can actively help create more sales. If the business, instead, has a problem with too many people contacting them via phone, then they may need a website to help manage their inquiries.

In other words, the website must act as a valuable tool that helps them fix their current problems, issues, and challenges. If you want to sell websites with ease, you must create websites that address and solve essential business problems.

"But isn't a nice design valuable?"

To address this question, we'll use an example.

It's prehistoric times, and food isn't easy to come by. A caveman is hungry and needs food. One day, the caveman encounters a cave-to-cave salesman selling fishing nets. The salesman shows off two nets: the first net looks very basic, but the net fabric is made of sturdy material. The second net is beautifully-crafted from rare materials, but the net fabric is made of flimsy material—in fact, the caveman can even see where the net is starting to tear. Now, which fishing net do you think the caveman will choose?

If he wants to catch any fish, let's hope he picks the first option.

And what about the salesman? He needs to sell more nets so he can eat as well. If he hopes to sell more nets to the cavepeople, which type of net should he continue selling?

The answer is obvious: the net that actually helps people catch fish. Not only will he have happy customers, but it's also likely they will tell their friends, which will bring him more customers.

If he continues to sell the net made of the flimsy material, word will spread that his nets are worthless. He won't make more sales, and he may have to face an angry mob of cave people—timber clubs in hands—who want their money back.

This example illustrates why smart web designers should focus on building a valuable business tool. They avoid building websites that just look good but do nothing.

Also, keep in mind, it's easy (and cheap) to buy websites that look good and do nothing already. You can go hire someone for $100 on Upwork to build a simple WordPress site or pay $20 to download a site theme. I know this is true because I used to be that guy on Upwork getting paid $100!

If you want to attract great clients and get paid well, don't get bogged down in coding languages and fancy design. Instead, focus on building a website that solves business problems.

People Pay for Value

As we witnessed during Dave's interaction with Angela, business owners care most about their top business needs.

Angela had an obvious pain point: she needed to find a better way to manage phone calls so that she could free up her time and run her business.

And thanks to the advice she received from her friend, Angela already had an idea of what could solve the problem. She just needed someone with the technical know-how to make these solutions a reality.

In other words, she was willing to pay someone who could help provide this value.

This value was something that Dave could have easily provided. All he had to do was put her business needs (freeing up her time) before his own (winning a competition) and be willing to take on something (copywriting) that he hadn't previously offered as a service.

If Dave focused on providing more value, instead of just design, he likely would have had a different outcome.

Fox Web School Student Case Study

Isaac O. increases his monthly income by 1,600%

Before joining Fox Web School in 2019, Isaac was struggling to make it as a web design freelancer.

Earlier in his design career, he was selling websites for $300 to $500 a piece. He would spend weeks finishing each website, making sure each one was technically perfect.

In a good month, he'd make $800. In a not-so-good month, he made much less.

He felt frustrated, but he was determined to make more money. So he stuck with the small projects, assuming that he would land bigger projects eventually.

After a few more months of struggling, Isaac decided to take a chance and join Fox Web School. With the knowledge he gained from the school, he experienced a complete shift in his mentality.

Two months after joining the program, he sold a single page for $750, more than *doubling* the price he used to charge for an *entire website*.

More impressively, he was also able to charge the same amount for a single page he created for a past client. When he had worked with that client previously, he had only charged $150.

So, what did Isaac learn that allowed him to charge five times as much for a web page than he did in the past? He learned how to think in terms of building valuable websites. He stopped building websites that just looked good and focused on building websites that actually solved problems and made a real difference to his clients.

Four months after joining the school, Isaac had made rapid progress. He had moved up to selling a larger website for $4,850 and another for $8,000, all within two days of each other. He was finally able to land high-paying clients.

He was now making $12,850 a month—a 1,600% increase from his previous $800.

"I've learned to pick the right businesses that not only had the budget for these projects, but would also reap the most for their investment. Also, they tend to be much more pleasant to work with," wrote Isaac. "I still have more struggles and obstacles I will have to overcome. But that's a good sign because that means there's more available to me."

Isaac is an example of one of our best students, but these types of changes are possible for anyone who switches from building websites that just *look* good to websites that make a real difference.

Always Speak the Language of Value

So far, I have made it a point to emphasize the fact that design and technical skills alone will not be enough to persuade a business owner to both hire you and pay you a decent price.

If you are an experienced web designer, you may be feeling a little disheartened. After all, you put so much time and effort into learning about the technical side of web design. Was that all for nothing?

The answer is no, as long as you remember to speak the language of value. If you can show how your technical expertise can provide value to a business, then you will always be an in-demand designer.

And if you're a new designer, don't feel discouraged about not knowing everything there is to know about web design. You will always have the ability to learn new skills, but your mindset will give you a leg up on even the most experienced designers. If you start with the right mindset first and pick up the technical skills as you take action, you can do very well in a short amount of time.

Mindset Shift Recap:

❶ Sell a result, not a website. A website is only ever a tool.
❷ Business owners always care most about their core business needs; not design, coding or technical aspects.
❸ The market pays you for the value you create; not your time, effort, background, or education.

CHAPTER 4
IF YOU THINK LIKE A BUSINESS OWNER, YOU WILL SUCCEED

If you think only like a web designer, you will fail.

In this final mindset chapter, I want to discuss one more key concept for running a profitable web design business. If you take this on board, it will significantly help you make huge progress in a very short amount of time. And once it clicks, you will find it easy to use.

That concept is this: always think first as a business owner, not as a web designer.

When you think like a business owner first, you always get better results, and you will:

- Understand exactly what to focus on when talking to business owners
- Be able to get the attention of business owners and build a connection fast
- Be able to uncover problems they have and how badly they need them fixed
- And (most importantly) know how to make a great deal for them (and for you) and persuade them to take action right away

To effectively sell web design, you need to think like a business owner.

When you think only as a web designer, things can go wrong very fast. You often miss out on great projects because you weren't on the same wavelength as the client. Many web designers lose deals like this every day.

The problem with thinking as a web designer is that you focus on all the wrong things. You are talking about code and design when the business owner wants to hear about solutions and results. You overlook discovering their problems so you can instead discuss layout and features. This puts your skills and interests above the business owner's needs and wants. And it rarely works.

To win more website deals at a much higher price, you need to instead develop the perspective of seeing things as a business owner. If you can do this, you will succeed.

◆◆◆

See Life Through Their Eyes

To think like a business owner, first, you must learn to see life from their angle.

For example, put on your business-owner glasses and pretend that you own a chain of highly-profitable barbershops. You started with one, but have since opened four additional locations, with plans to expand into a nearby city.

It is a Monday morning, and you are sitting down to plan out the week ahead. Even though it is the first official workday of your week, you are already feeling burned out because of how busy the prior week was and how little time off you had over the weekend to recover.

You take a sip of coffee and try to focus on the immediate tasks at hand: which staff members are working, which staff members need their shifts covered because they are sick or on holiday, what supplies you need to order with consideration to how much inventory you already have on the way, and then, of course, there is the matter of calculating payroll. These are just the main tasks for Monday morning! You likely have another dozen things lined up for the afternoon and maybe even late into the evening.

To say you have no time for any distractions or nonsense is putting it mildly!

As you start into this work, you notice a new email at the top of your inbox. It is from someone you do not know, but somehow it did not go to your spam folder.

You open the email and begin to read.

> *Hi Mr. Martinez,*
>
> *My name is Michelle, and I am a web designer.*
>
> *I have contacted you because I found your website on google and have noticed the design is out of date. I offer new modern websites at a great price that you can afford.*
>
> *I was hoping to talk to you right away to see what deal would be best for you.*
>
> *Would you be able to jump on a quick 20-minute call to discuss? Here is my number...*

You finish reading and stare at the email.

You think, *"Who is this person to tell me my website looks old and outdated? They don't know a thing about what my business does, let alone what issues we have right now.*

I have a million other more important things to do this week than to spend money on some fancy design. I need to get back to calculating payroll, I need to order more supplies, I have some staff out sick today, I need to...

Now more frustrated, you close the tab.

Now let me ask you this: as a business owner, does this type of email seem important or annoying? You're being lectured by some random stranger online.

Chances are you would do exactly what this business owner did—just hit delete (and maybe block).

Ricky Thinks Like a Business Owner

A few weeks after the first meeting with Pete, the owner of the renovations business, Ricky was ready to show him the newly updated website.

The website had all of the features they discussed, came in under budget, and looked professional and on point. To say that Pete was thrilled with the results would be an understatement.

As a way to express his gratitude, he offered to take Ricky to lunch at his favorite Thai spot across the street.

Ricky had never heard of this particular restaurant, and it didn't look like much from the outside. But after entering the restaurant, Ricky was delighted by the warm and colorful interior and the aroma coming from the kitchen.

After waiting for a few minutes, he took his first bite of massaman curry.

This food is so delicious, Ricky thought to himself. *How have I never heard of this place before?*

He looked around and noticed that besides two men at a corner table, he and Pete were the only customers.

He glanced at the clock. It was noon.

"This curry is so delicious. It's surprising to see this place so empty at lunchtime," said Ricky.

"Yeah, it's a hidden gem," Pete said. "The owners are nice people. I've never seen them advertise anywhere, though."

Pete continued, "But last time I was in here, the owner mentioned that his son had just graduated from university and was going to help them run the business."

"Oh," said Ricky. "I think I may know some ways to help them get more clients."

Ricky's mind was racing with ideas of how a website could boost their business: online ordering, photos of the food and interior, a way to book parties or events, a place for reviews.

Ricky continued, "Do you know how I could get in touch with the owner's son?"

Pete smiled. "I bet you I can get an email address," he winked. Pete got up and walked toward the register.

Now that he was thinking like a business owner, Ricky saw opportunities everywhere he went to help improve other businesses. It was no longer just, "is their current website outdated," but rather, "is there a way to use web design to help improve their business?"

He first thought about what a business owner might need and then presented himself as the person to help them make it happen. Ricky was now viewing web design as just a tool, which meant that he first focused on any potential to help a business improve.

This mindset is what gets fast results, and it will get him a ton of potential leads.

◆◆◆

A Different Approach

When thinking of the barber scenario earlier, I want to pose another question:

If you were the owner of that business, what would make you want to respond to Michelle's cold email? What could Michelle possibly say that would make you take time out of your hectic day to reply?

From what you've learned so far, you know that Michelle should address *what is most important to the business owner*. If she only talks about design or website features, most business owners won't care—those items are a low priority when compared to their many other current problems.

So if Michelle wants to get a response, she should focus on what is likely to matter most.

Even if Michelle did not know the current problems that the barbershop owner was facing, she could still frame her services as helpful and relevant to what the owner is most likely to want for their business in the future.

Let's say that Michelle crafted this email instead:

Hi Mr. Martinez,
I live in your area and have several friends who go to your barbershop frequently.

It is great to see the progress you are making with the business, and I know that recently you have started to expand even more with several new locations.

The reason for my email is that I wanted to see if I could help you with this growth.

It seems there is a lot of potential with your current website and online systems to make your life easier by reducing the work involved with handling new customers' questions and bookings.

I also think, depending on your goals, that we can look at how the website could help the future growth of the business. There are several things I have spotted that I could do to help free up your time, while improving sales.

I would love to send you some more info on this, or if possible, have a quick call tomorrow at a time that is good for you. Would you be free to talk for 15 minutes in the morning or afternoon?

Thanks,

Michelle

999-1111-000

Most of us would be much more likely to reply to the second email than the first.

Why? Because Michelle focused on how her services would potentially help the business in a way that is very relevant and valuable. She talked about reducing workload, improving sales, and helping with future growth. To put it simply: she focused on the most important areas that any business owner is likely and willing to spend money on.

Michelle wasn't trying to sell herself or her design experience; she was trying to sell a desirable SOLUTION. And this is what will get the attention and interest of business owners.

◆◆◆

Mindset Comes First. Action Comes Second.

As we draw our Mindset chapters to a close, we're almost ready to jump into the next section: Taking Action.

We covered mindset first before taking action because, without having the right mindset, you can take a lot of action and still fail, which is why many people work hard but get nowhere.

Luckily for you, you now have a great mindset that will make the difference in your approach. It has been proven to work for many others, and as long as you use the mindset principles outlined in this book, you will succeed, too.

As you read through the upcoming chapters, remember these proven mindset principles. When you think in the right way, any action you take is going to be 10 to100 times more effective. Having a great mindset is a small difference that makes all the difference.

So congratulations—after reading the above Mindset section, you are one giant step closer to becoming a successful web design freelancer.

Ready to keep going and take some action together?

If so, great! Let's get started.

◆◆◆

Mindset Shift Recap:

❶ Sell a result, not a website. A website is only ever a tool.

❷ Business owners always care most about their core business needs; not design, coding or technical aspects.

❸ The market pays you for the value you create; not your time, effort, background, or education.

❹ If you think like a business owner, you will succeed. If you think only like a web designer, you will fail.

TAKING ACTION

CHAPTER 5

BECOME A PROFESSIONAL PROBLEM SOLVER

Make this your number one priority.

Welcome to the first Taking Action chapter! I hope that you are now feeling much more confident in your ability to thrive as a web design freelancer.

In these Action chapters, we will take a high-level overview of the steps you need to take to launch a successful business. You can use this overview to help with your web design freelance business or something else entirely—the lessons you'll learn here can apply to any business in any field.

While the previous chapters focused on embracing a new way of thinking, these pages will provide you with actionable advice for your new business (once you have adopted the necessary mindset shift, of course).

Which brings us to our first—and most essential—step: become a professional problem solver.

We have already learned that business owners always focus on their core business needs, and that results are what matters.

But to provide results, you must first learn how to solve problems.

Businesses Have Plenty of Problems

All businesses face problems, even extremely profitable companies. No matter the type of business, there is always going to be something they want to maintain or, better yet, improve.

You do not need to have experience running your own business to see this. Think back to any job you ever had, and you can likely remember many problems the boss was dealing with at different times.

If there is one thing that every business will always need, it's a person who can spot and solve big problems that hold a business back.

Let's say you are the owner of Gary's Go-Karts, a popular indoor go-kart track located a few minutes outside of a mid-sized city. The business is located on the side of a busy road, and it has been doing well for years. But from day one, there have always been some common problems.

On any given night, you might have to deal with people showing up late for their bookings or people not showing up at all. You may have to deal with racers breaking some rules on the track, ensure the food and drink area is clean, keep karts maintained correctly, and deal with any crashes that might happen.

All these problems are annoying but also expected. As the experienced owner of a go-kart business, you will know what to do when these issues arise and how to keep things running smoothly.

But let's imagine a very different problem—you are running out of new customers.

Unfortunately, last month a new highway was built, and now fewer and fewer people are driving by your location. You have noticed your customer numbers drop off, and each racing night, there are more empty go-karts.

Now the problems of dealing with late bookings and go-kart maintenance seem smaller and smaller. The big problem of "not enough customers" is all you can think about now.

Since your business has always done well in the past, you are unsure of how to deal with this new problem. You know everything there is to know about go-karting, but you have no idea how to attract new customers.

As you start to brainstorm, you may wonder: what can I do?

...

Should I build a bigger sign out front?
Although the current sign is huge, it isn't attracting more people.

...

Should I run a deal on Groupon?
Wait, I already tried that before, and it didn't bring in any customers.

...

Should I buy some radio ads?
I know they are expensive, and I wonder if they will even be effective.

...

Should I try online marketing?
But how does that even work, and where should I start???

What this business needs most is not someone who is another expert at all things related to go-karting. The owner already has extensive go-karting expertise, and this hasn't helped solve this new problem. Instead, the business needs someone who is an expert problem solver. They need someone who can see their problems in a new light and get the business back on track.

And they need this person *right now*.

◆◆◆

Solving Problems Is Your Mission

If your goal is to have total control over your time and financial life, you must make problem-solving your mission. This must be your mission because professional problem solvers create business ideas and projects that work. They build solutions that are a win-win for everyone involved and are usually very profitable too. The world always rewards those people who can add value and solve big problems. It really is that simple!

From now on, you need to think of yourself as a professional problem solver, not a web designer. Designing websites is a part of what you DO, but not who you ARE.

That's right, you are a solution-finding problem solver on a mission to help businesses get better. Selling solutions is what gets you paid, and a website is simply one tool (sound familiar?) you can use to solve the problems you find. Web design is just the next skill you are learning on your journey to becoming the best problem solver you can be.

Let's see how this looks in action. Think back to the problem Gary has with his GoKart business. The big problem? The go-kart track needs more customers to continue to operate and stay profitable. If they don't find more customers, they will likely go out of business sooner rather than later.

Now let's say you happen to land a meeting with Gary. You have a 30-minute conversation where you ask him a bunch of questions to understand what is going on in his business. He explains everything about his business, including its new big problem, and you can tell he is in a tough situation and badly needs help.

So, what do you suggest as a solution?

If you don't know the answer right now, that is okay. This is just an example, and you would need to talk to a real business owner to know for sure.

But for this example, it turns out that Gary hasn't been doing much online marketing or sales at all. You ask him why that is, and he tells you he just never saw the need to get business from the internet when there were so many cars driving past his business every day.

Your next step is to take a look at what online presence he has, if any. You find out that it only consists of an outdated Facebook page from when the business first opened, along with a basic website someone on his team threw together within a day. He says they occasionally have people message them on Facebook to ask about opening hours, and they receive maybe an email or two from the website each month.

You now have two parts of the puzzle: a big problem that needs to be solved quickly (not enough sales) and a great potential way to help solve it (improve Gary's online marketing).

Things are looking very good for your new career in problem-solving.

With this new information, you now do some research to show Gary what is possible.

You find a similar go-kart business in another city and notice they have a great website, complete with great photos and racing videos. It has the opening hours and booking details listed, and a section on how to book parties and corporate events. They even have a racing club member section with race day events and the fastest track lap records.

The whole website looks very fun and exciting, but it is also expertly designed to help create new sales and attract new customers. You can clearly see how something similar would be very effective for Gary's business.

With this in mind, you share your plan with Gary to demonstrate all the great things about his own business that can be shared online to improve his sales. On the website, he can show his race track, explain why they are a great place to come to and have some fun, and how easy it can be to book a race night. This way, Gary starts to see the website not just as a "thing," but as a valuable part of his business.

Your website solution is now looking more and more like the best way to solve Gary's big problem. It directly relates to what the problem is, it has worked for others, and you can show him a clear way to make your solution work. A deal is now looking very likely.

This is how problem solvers both pitch and sell solutions to businesses every day. They find other people's big problems and then use their creative skills to come up with a solution.

While Gary's Go-Karting is just one example in this book, there are millions of real businesses out there right now with problems like this. These businesses are in every country, in thousands of different niches with millions of different problems, but they all have this in common—they all badly need someone who can spot and solve those problems.

If you don't believe me, you can check the stats on the millions of businesses that close every single year. While businesses go under for a variety of reasons, they all close because of a big problem they were never able to solve. They needed a problem solver like you who could help them, but they didn't find one in time.

So always remember—to be in demand and to make it easy to find well-paying clients, you must focus on solving big problems. The more you pay attention to what matters most, and the more you get the type of results that matter most, the bigger and more profitable your web design business will be.

"What big business problem can I solve?"—This is a key mindset for you to succeed in business.

♦♦♦

SIDE NOTE: PROBLEM SOLVING MAKES YOU RICH

At the moment, we are focusing on just web design, but problem-solving is at the heart of any successful business. If you look at the top businesses or entrepreneurs in any industry, they are all highly-effective problem solvers.

Elon Musk solved the problem of cheaper space travel, better—and more fun—electric cars, and with PayPal, the problem of how to send money online.

Jeff Bezos solved the problem of buying products online safely, reliably, and with ease.

Sara Blakely solved the problem of making clothes that are both comfortable and appealing to women. She went from teaching herself how to sew to becoming a billionaire within a few years.

The pattern is always consistent—if someone is a big name in business and has amassed a lot of personal wealth, it's very likely because they are expert problem solvers.

Now, this might seem daunting at first. How can you possibly start solving problems on this level?

The trick is to start small. Learn how to solve small problems, and then move on to slightly larger problems, and so on. Problem-solving is a skill, and if you start now, you will be surprised by just how quickly you can improve it.

Which brings us back to web design: web design freelancing is one of the best areas to start learning entrepreneurship because it teaches you *how* to become a problem solver.

As a web design freelancer, you get to help real businesses that have real problems and pain points. Web design requires mastering skills like creative thinking, communication, sales, marketing, and value creation—which are all skills you need to be an expert problem solver.

As long as you focus on building real-world skills through web design and not just making pointless websites that only look good, you can learn valuable problem-solving skills in a short amount of time. As you get better at solving problems, you can tackle bigger problems and land bigger clients.

This increased ability to decipher problems is exactly why many top web designers don't stay within the field of web design forever. Instead, they use their newfound skills to move into other niches and industries where they can solve even bigger problems and create more value.

If you want to create wealth and freedom with web design, problem-solving should be your top focus.

♦♦♦

Taking Action Recap:

❶ Become a professional problem solver. Make this your number one priority.

CHAPTER 6
HAVE CONVERSATIONS THAT FOCUS ON PROBLEMS AND FRUSTRATIONS

Don't just guess; listening is essential.

As we saw in the last chapter, it is essential to become a professional problem solver to be successful.

If you're thinking, *okay, but* how *do I do that exactly?*

Don't worry. We've got you covered.

In this second Action chapter, we will focus on the strategies you can use to uncover problems, frustrations, and needs.

◆◆◆

GET YOUR INFORMATION DIRECTLY FROM THE SOURCE

If you want to solve problems, you need to find problems. This is obvious. But how do you start to go about finding them?

The examples of Dave and Ricky trying to help Pete's renovation business at the beginning of this book give us a massive clue.

When Dave went to meet Pete, he already had a proposal prepared to present to him. Pete even tried to tell Dave about his business woes, but Dave didn't listen. He believed he already *knew* everything about Pete's business and exactly what Pete wanted. He was wrong.

Ricky, on the other hand, had a conversation with Pete first, before ever considering how he would design the website. He allowed Pete to tell him all about his problems and frustrations before ever suggesting a possible website solution. He first listened and made sure that he understood.

The lesson? The best way to learn a business's problems is by speaking directly with the business owner—never by making assumptions. Before trying to sell a solution, you need to first fully understand the situation.

Not understanding the situation is a common problem that sets back many web designers. In the rush to make progress, many web design freelancers try to tell business owners what their problems are—often without knowing much about the business owner or the business itself. This almost never works.

When you try to guess problems, you often guess wrong. Even if you guess right, it's likely you still don't know enough about the problem to fully understand it. When you don't fully understand a problem (or you guessed wrong in the first place), it is nearly impossible to solve.

With this mindset, you will probably try to sell a solution that the business owner knows does not match their actual problem. They will either ignore you or tell you nicely, "No deal."

So what is a better approach?

You need to begin any potential sale by focusing on getting the business owner to tell you exactly what their problems are.

You need to understand what big problems they have, how these problems are impacting them, what areas of the business they are damaging, and the stress that this is causing. You want to gather all the details you can use to understand what exactly is going on and how it feels for the business owner.

The thing is, business owners already know their problems. They can see if sales are down. They know if they aren't getting new customers. They can tell they are wasting a lot of time replying to emails.

They don't need you to guess anything.

Instead, they need someone they can trust to listen to them and someone who will actually care.

Gain Permission

Another crucial thing to note when it comes to problem-solving is the need to gain permission *before* attempting to solve a problem.

As we check back in with Dave, we find him frustrated, but still determined. He slowly realizes that he must offer more than just a fast and visually appealing website—he must build a website that functions as a useful tool. He starts to keep an eye out for any potential opportunities.

One day, Dave is busy researching local businesses. He takes a break to check his phone and notices a missed call and a voicemail from a few hours earlier.

He dials his voicemail and listens to the following message:

> *Hi Dave, Jamie here from Dr. Brown's office. We noticed your contact prescription is about to expire, and you didn't schedule a follow-up appointment the last time you were in the office. Give us a call back, and we'll get you in for an eye exam. Thanks!*

Dave returns the call, but the practice is already closed for the day. He navigates to their website to see if he can make an appointment virtually. He notices they don't have an online scheduler and realizes this could be a potential area of opportunity for his optometrist.

The following week, he goes in for his appointment. As the exam is coming to an end and Dr. Brown is writing Dave a new prescription, Dave begins chatting with him about his website.

Intrigued by what Dave suggested, Dr. Brown asks Dave to come back the following Monday to discuss more details about a potential website update.

Dave is thrilled. He finally feels like he is on the right path.

During their meeting, all is going well. Dave is doing everything he can to explain his website update as a solution to the problems Dr. Brown shared during their initial conversation.

He feels like he is getting a positive reaction from Dr. Brown, so he decides to take things a step further.

"Dr. Brown, if I may, there is one other thing I want to suggest. I noticed the design of your website is extremely outdated. I could update your site to have a more modern look," says Dave. "I'm not sure who you hired to create this site, but it looks like a child made it," Dave finishes, laughing.

Unfortunately, he's the only one laughing.

"I made the site, Dave," replies Dr. Brown.

Dave falls silent.

…

Can you say *awkward*?

This scenario illustrates why you always need to gain permission before attempting to solve a problem. The doctor already knows his website doesn't look very professional, but Dave gains nothing by telling him so. In fact, when Dave says so, he loses trust as a "problem solver." Instead, he now looks like a "problem maker"—and no one likes those.

So always keep this in mind: no one likes to hear they are wrong or stupid, even if you're talking about an area outside of their expertise. Always ask what the problem might be, instead of assuming. Never jump in and start telling people what problems you think they have.

◆◆◆

MORE PROBLEMS, MORE MONEY

You've likely heard the saying "more money, more problems" (especially if you're a Notorious B.I.G. fan). But the opposite can also be the case for a website design freelancer (or any business owner) if you are the one who can *solve* the problems.

If you want to make more money and land better projects, you need to be able to identify more potential pain points you can solve. The more problems you can solve, the more money you will be able to make.

To recap: listening is vital.

Always have a conversation with the business owner to learn the business problems directly from the source. Never assume a problem exists, and always gain permission before attempting to solve a problem.

Also, don't forget that more problems = more money, so always listen to other potential areas of improvement.

Taking Action Recap:

❶ Become a professional problem solver. Make this your number one priority.

❷ Have conversations that focus on problems and frustrations. Don't just guess; listening is essential.

CHAPTER 7
Start Where Your Trust Is Highest

Use your current connections to start right away.

At this point, you should realize the importance of becoming a professional problem solver. With this approach, you are much more likely to achieve success than other freelancers who do not understand this.

But this is still only half the puzzle. What you need to think of next is what type of clients are most likely to want to work with you right now.

As an aspiring web design freelancer, you're likely choosing this path because you want increased flexibility, control over your time, and a higher earning potential. These are all great and achievable goals, but at the start, many aspiring designers often take the wrong approach. The mistake many people make is focusing right away on landing big, high-ticket projects with large companies.

Now, while these projects can be great, they are NOT the projects you want to go for first. Going after big projects in the beginning is a very common mistake, and it can cost some freelancers months or years of wasted efforts. They think the best way to make money as fast as possible is to go right for the biggest jobs they could possibly get. It sounds good in theory, but it rarely, if ever, works.

The reason it doesn't work is that these companies are very unlikely to trust you at the moment—even if you can help them. They don't know who you are, they can't see who else you have worked with, and they can't tell if you are capable of helping them. And since they see no logical way for them to trust you, they simply choose not to work with you.

This brings us to a core selling principle: to sell anything to anyone, you must first establish trust. If someone can't trust you, then they won't ever buy from you. Even when people want to buy, or *need* to buy, they will still only do so with someone they trust.

Every sale must start with trust. This matters a lot when selling websites.

With this in mind, let's look at who you should be working with first and what common mistakes to avoid.

♦♦♦

"I Came Across Your Website Online..."

As a freelancer, you are going to be responsible for getting your own clients. You are not backed by an agency or a support system that will bring clients to you. You must seek them out on your own.

This means you will have to learn how to sell.

This reality can be scary for a new freelancer. Ultimately, clients equal income, and if freelancing is your only form of income, it can put a lot of pressure on you financially. Many people view sales as an impossible challenge, but you can learn how to sell effectively to anyone if you use the right approach.

Consider this common scenario.

Suppose you live in a small town in Scotland and you have just started your web design business. This business is your only source of income, and you desperately need to land your first client. After some research into potential "large" clients, you've set your sights on the top law firms in New York City. You think, "*If I can just get a major law firm to be my client, then I will be on my way.*"

With this goal in mind, you start plotting how to get to speak to a top decision-maker at one of these firms. You decide to look for problems on their website in the hopes of getting their attention and possibly a call.

After a quick look, you have already found quite a few areas you could help improve, but you keep searching because you feel that the more problems you find, the higher your chances of getting a response will be. After a few hours, you have a detailed list of potential clients and all their current website issues.

Feeling confident in what you've discovered, you turn your attention to finding the right contact information. The law partners are listed on the "About Us" page, but when you call, you realize you won't be able to speak to anyone without knowing the correct phone extension.

Instead, you decide to fill out a form on their website and hope for the best. You craft an extremely well-written email that poses you as an expert problem-solver. You feel confident as you hit "send."

Unfortunately, you don't hear back within a few days. Weeks go by and, still, no response.

Where did things go wrong?

First off, this sucks. I know because I did this a lot when I first started, and it was very frustrating. Not getting a response always stings, especially after you spent hours writing great emails, only to get nothing.

It wasn't until later that it became very obvious why it wasn't working—there was no trust.

And when there is no trust, there is not likely to be a sale. It is a waste of time.

You could be saying all the right things, focusing on areas they badly need to hire someone to help with. They might even have a ton of money ready to spend on fixing the problem, but if they don't trust you or see a way they can trust you, they will still pass on your offer for help.

This is annoying when you first start, but it is something you have to be aware of. It is just too risky for a business to rely on you to help them if they can't yet trust you.

Consider it from the side of the large law firm. The law firm has important clients they represent, they have a strong reputation, and they have a lot of potential money and business on the line. Yet you are cold-emailing them from another country with no prior experience or results, *hoping* that they trust you to fix all their big problems. It doesn't work.

This will often result in freelancers saying things like *cold emailing never works,* or *cold calling sucks, people just hang up on you.* But this isn't true! Cold calling and cold emailing can work great—people use them every day to sell all types of products and services. But you must be able to show them some way they can trust you to make it work. Otherwise, it's pointless.

Right now, you may be thinking, "*But people can trust me. I am a great person."* I am sure you are, but the problem is when people don't already know *you,* they have to decide if they trust your *business* instead. It isn't personal.

THE DIFFERENCE BETWEEN TRUSTING A PERSON AND TRUSTING A BUSINESS

When people are deciding to spend money on a new business service or product, they need to see that they can trust the business itself. You might be the most trustworthy salesperson ever, but once you are selling a service to a business, they also need to see they can trust that service independent of you. They want to see that it's proven, safe, and reliable. They want proof that it does what you say it will. If your potential buyer can't trust your business, then it doesn't matter how much they might like you—there still won't be any deal.

Think of it this way: would you get on a flight with a friendly pilot if the plane looked like it was about to fall apart the moment it took off? Probably not.

Would you feel safe driving a car full-speed on a highway after someone told you the car was made a hundred years ago and they hoped it still worked well? I highly doubt it.

It is the exact same with web design—business owners will only trust you when they can also trust your web design services. The more they trust your web design services, the more they will trust you as a provider as well. It works both ways. You must show a business owner they can trust your website design skills before they will even start thinking about a possible deal. No amount of personal charm or charisma can help if your actual business looks too risky.

THE CHICKEN AND THE EGG DILEMMA

If you want to start a new web design business, but you first need to be able to show completed website projects to a business owner to get them to trust you, then how can you ever actually get started?

It seems like it might be impossible, but there is a way.

The answer is to first work with the people who are already likely to trust you. You must begin by focusing on people who can trust you personally while you build up your business results. Then, when you have enough business results, personal trust isn't as important because potential clients can see that what you are selling is trustworthy on its own.

Yes, the best way to sell big website deals as fast as possible is by first building real website results so that businesses can see and trust that your web design services will help them, too.

If you think about this, you can see how it works in your own life, too. You would probably feel safe going to a restaurant where you don't know the owner, but where you can see hundreds of great reviews online. Once you can trust the actual business itself, then it doesn't matter who the owner is. You just needed to know the place was a safe choice.

To succeed in web design, you need to start by creating that feeling with potential clients first—that feeling where they can rely on you to help their business get results. You must show them that they can trust you and that, by working with you, they can get to a better place.

The best way to start creating this level of trust now is by taking on some quick projects for people who know you personally and who would be willing to give you a shot.

So, Who is Likely to Trust You Right Now?

The answer is, lots of people! Your family. Your friends. Your personal connections. The people with whom you attended university or school. People from the past jobs you might have had or places you used to live. People you know who run businesses that you talk to or visit often. People who live in your area. People who go to the same sports club or a gym as you.

Basically, anyone who is connected to you in any way may already trust you.

It might be a strong connection, like your best friend's sister, or a weaker connection, like that person you talk to at yoga sometimes, who has a cousin with a small business in the next city over.

There are three main things you should look for in a potential client as a beginner:

1. Are they likely to trust you more than they would trust a total stranger?
2. Do they have a real business?
3. Is it possible to reach out to them?

And that is it!

If they have a real business, are someone you can contact, and there is an established connection, then it's a perfect place for you to start.

Here are examples of the type of people that were first-time clients for some of my students:

- The owner of their local gym
- A person they met at a local business course
- Their former boss
- Their dad's business
- The owner of a nearby restaurant
- Their family dentist
- A friend of a friend
- A business owner they messaged from a local Facebook group
- Someone they met at a local sports event

If these all seem like a very easy way to get your first client, it is because they are. There is no need to go for the hardest possible deals when you first start. Make it easy on yourself and reach out to those who already trust you. You already know some people, and they know people too. Use the network that you already have to get your first deal or two.

Keep in mind, though, that this is only a starting strategy. It is not meant to last forever (and it won't). It's just the best place to get your first few deals while you build some real results you can use to create trust with bigger actors later. In short, it is the most effective way to kickstart your business and build the foundation you will later need to land much bigger deals.

With our tale of two web designers, we already saw both Ricky and Dave use this approach. They leveraged their personal connections and other opportunities when first starting as freelancers. Dave met Pete through a university buddy, whereas Ricky was introduced to him through Pete's nephew, who was a friend of a coworker. Pete helped Ricky connect to the Thai restaurant owner's son, while Dave's sister introduced him to her photographer friend. Reaching out to connections is how most of the top web designers get going— and it's fast and easy.

◆◆◆

To Work for Free, or to Get Paid Right Away

A question I often get asked is, *"should I work for free when first starting?"*

My advice is to take a long-term approach.

Look at your first few projects as an investment in your own business. Do you want to focus on just making fast but small money right now, or do you want to focus first on building the best business you can now, so that it can be highly profitable later? I hope it's the second.

The problem with focusing on getting paid right away is it will often lead you down the wrong path. Sometimes the clients who are willing to pay you right away are not the best types of jobs to take. These clients often just want someone to do random work, but it won't be the type of work where you get to build up your problem-solving skillset. You will do one project, make a few dollars, and be right back where you started—it doesn't go anywhere.

If, instead, you focus on getting the best results possible with your first few projects, then it won't be long until your prices increase very quickly. Maybe you work for free, or maybe you don't, but make sure that you focus your first few projects on showing how valuable your work can be. Once you have just a few past projects where you can show how you helped a business significantly, you won't ever struggle to find paying clients and land profitable website deals. Once you have a solid website business foundation in place, things get a lot easier. Focus on results first and profits later.

◆◆◆

Make a List of People Who Trust You the Most

Since this is the Taking Action section of this guide, let's get into some practical steps you can take right away. I will introduce real actions you can do right now to begin creating a profitable web design business.

Grab a pen and paper and make a list of all of the people who trust you.

Think of everyone you know, either directly or through someone else. Think of every business, group, club, society, or event you have visited or been involved with in the last few years. Then, list the people you see from time to time and anyone you have connected with randomly in the past.

Don't consider anything else when making this list other than whether or not these people are more likely to trust you than a complete stranger. They might be your best buddy, or they might be someone you have never met, but who happens to know someone you know.

As long as they are likely to trust you more than they would a total stranger, that is enough to make the list.

Once you have completed this list, pick at least one person to reach out to about your new web design business. Let them know what you are trying to do and ask if they can connect you to any business owner they know who might need your help. It might be someone they know who owns a business, helps manage a business, or who knows another business owner personally. Maybe they themselves own a business, which, of course, would be ideal.

You can say something like this:

Hi,

I just wanted to let you know I have started a web design business and am looking for 1 or 2 potential clients to help. If you know of anyone who needs help growing their business or getting more sales, please let me know.

Also, since this is one of my first projects, I will offer a fair price for quality work, and be sure to get them the best results I can. If you know of someone you could put me in touch with, it would be greatly appreciated. Thanks.

Keep reaching out to people on your list until you find your first opportunity to help a business. You never know who has a problem you can solve.

♦♦♦

Taking Action Recap:

❶ Become a professional problem solver. Make this your number one priority.

❷ Have conversations that focus on problems and frustrations. Don't just guess; listening is essential.

❸ Start where your trust is highest. Use your current connections to start right away.

CHAPTER 8

Leverage Your Past Results to Land Bigger Projects

More past results = more future sales.

As you learned in the last chapter, reaching out to those in your network can be a great way to get started as a web design freelancer. Starting where your trust is highest is the quickest way to begin building real valuable results. Having just a few of these results is going to allow you to quickly attract the attention and interest of business owners.

Even if the initial projects you are taking on are small, you are still creating *real* results. By solving actual problems that business owners care about, you show other businesses the value of working with you. Instead of trying to pitch fancy design features (that, as we have shown, rarely mean anything to a business owner), you can now show results, which can equate to real change for a business.

Pitching a website based on design features is where most freelancers go wrong—many get stuck building cheaper websites forever because they don't know how to show *why* they are worth more. Every time they finish a project, they are right back where they started, hoping that the next project somehow goes better.

When you learn to leverage your past results, though, you won't have this problem. You can learn to grab the attention of any business owner and demonstrate why a website can help their business. You no longer have to only focus on people who already know or trust you. You can be proactive and go directly after whatever type of deals and profits you desire.

In short, learning to leverage your past results means a lot more opportunities to sell more projects and a significantly higher chance of landing larger deals. Knowing how to use your past results is going to allow you to see rapid progress and be able to increase your prices. If you want to grow a profitable web design business, you must start first by building some real results.

With this in mind, let's see exactly how to best leverage any past projects you have done.

◆◆◆

LET YOUR PAST RESULTS SPEAK FOR THEMSELVES

Say you've landed and completed your first web design project. It was a small project—a simple one-page website for your local coffee shop. The project went well, and even though it was your first website, the owner is happy with your results. Perfect.

Now, maybe you got paid $300 for this website, or maybe you did it for free—at this stage, it doesn't matter much. What does matter is how you now leverage that project to get bigger and better deals.

It's important to remember that business owners will only pay big money when they feel confident that you can get them big results. They need to see that you have solved similar problems to their own in the past and that you have a decent plan to do it again for them. They will want to hear specific examples of what you have done for businesses in the past and how you helped those businesses, which is why learning to leverage your past results in the right way is so important. You must be able to clearly show what you can do if you want to be successful.

To begin creating results, you must talk and think in terms of "what the website does" rather than "how the website looks." You need to forget about the design for now and focus on how websites solve problems.

When thinking about past projects, here are some questions to ask yourself:

- What business problems did you fix?
- What business solutions did you create?
- What value did you add to the business (how is it better than before)?
- Did you help the business grow (new sales, new customers, new deals, etc.)?
- Did you reduce the time, effort, or stress involved in running the business?
- How much was your work worth to this client and their business?

Once you can pinpoint results that you have achieved with past clients, you can use them to get the attention of other potential clients. Show how your websites make a difference and can be used to solve frustrating problems. Focus on how you can save them time, make them more money, grow their business, and get them the exact type of client they want.

A website is only worth what it can achieve for a business, and it's essential to see it from this perspective in order to understand how to get business owners to care about working with you.

Your websites are only ever going to be worth what a business owner is willing to pay for them. Business owners are likely going to pay 100 times more for what they badly need rather than something that just looks good.

So, before pitching your next client, start looking at what problems your websites have solved and the results you can accomplish. You must always think like a business owner and show how your website is a solution to their problems. This is what allows you to go from selling $300 websites to closing $10,000+ projects.

RICKY LEVERAGES PAST RESULTS, WHILE DAVE DOES NOT

As we check back in with Ricky, he is preparing to meet with Malee, the Thai restaurant owner's son. He is grateful to Pete for connecting him with a new potential client, but he knows that a mutual connection won't be enough to seal the deal. He instead needs to talk about the results his website can get for Malee's restaurant. He needs to show how he can help.

Since it has only been a couple of weeks since he completed Pete's website, Ricky probably will not yet be able to show that the new website he built has led to a significant boost in organic traffic or sales. But sales are just one part of how his website is designed to help Pete's business—there are many other areas he can use to show the value of his work.

He decides to focus on what Pete's website has already accomplished since the day it launched. While talking to Malee, Ricky makes sure to highlight the following accomplishments:

1. **The website builds trust with potential clients.**
   Before working with Ricky, Pete had trouble building trust with potential clients. Ricky helped fix this issue by adding content and information about Pete's business to the website. This content helps build trust among those who are seeking a renovation. New potential clients now feel more confident and secure when dealing with Pete.

2. **The website makes it easier to attract potential sales leads.**
   Ricky's new website has made it easier to attract potential sales leads. The website now walks people through exactly what information they need, and in the right order, to move towards contacting Pete about a project. It is like having a perfect sales pitch about Pete's business online, ready for anyone to use at any time of the day.

3. **The website reduces employee workload.**
   The new website even reduces the workload for Pete's team. They no longer get dozens of emails a week with questions, because the answers to these frequently asked questions are now on the website. Customers are now getting the right information faster, and Pete's team has more time to focus on helping their current clients to get the best customer care possible.

4. **The website was tailor-made for Pete's business.**
   Finally, Ricky explains that the website he built for Pete was specific to his problems and that any website he builds is unique to what is

needed to help that particular client. He also explains how each website is only ever a tool; and how this tool is used depends on the goals and challenges of his client.

Malee, the Thai restaurant owner's son, is impressed. He wanted someone who understands the needs of his business and who might be able to help him with his specific problems. Ricky's services are exactly what he needs. He decides to give Ricky a chance to see what he can do.

♦♦♦

On the flip side, when it comes to leveraging results, we see a huge missed opportunity for our struggling designer, Dave.

While Dave has the benefit of prior professional web design experience, he has yet to learn how to utilize his past results to gain new clients. Although he has the technical skills and knowhow, he is not focusing on the areas that matter most, and this makes him seem unsuitable to help any new potential client.

This communication problem comes from his past experience. While working for the software company, he always considered himself a web designer, never a problem-solver. So when it came time to branch out on his own, he was more concerned with highlighting the design and technical aspects of the websites in his portfolio, instead of business results. He has been focusing on design and code, while his potential clients wanted to see practical solutions and results.

This wasted leverage is a shame. Dave has more than enough skills to land profitable website deals. Unfortunately, when he only focuses on design features, very few business owners can see his potential. If only Dave had adopted a business owner's mindset, he would have been able to frame his past work as problem-solving tools, instead of non-essential expensive website designs.

Don't make the same mistakes as Dave. Always leverage your past results by focusing on a business's current needs, problems, and desires. You must always show what you can do to help them.

Once you apply what we have covered so far, things will start to click fast. When you can find problems that need solving and also show how you have already solved similar problems for others, you look like a very good option. You no longer look like an ordinary web designer selling the same type of designs. Instead, you are now something very different: a person who can solve big problems and move a business forward. Any business owner wants to work with this type of person.

◆◆◆

Mindset. Action. What's Next?

If you have made it to the end of this section, you are already many steps ahead of most web design freelancers. You are now thinking like a business owner instead of a web designer, and you have a practical list of proven strategies that you can use to create a profitable web design business.

Now, we're ready to jump into the final section: Parting Advice. These last few pieces of wisdom will help you beyond landing your first few clients, so that you can achieve long-lasting success in your web design business and beyond.

◆◆◆

Mindset Shift Recap:

❶ Sell a result, not a website. A website is only ever a tool.
❷ Business owners always care most about their core business needs; not design, coding or technical aspects.
❸ The market pays you for the value you create; not your time, effort, background, or education.
❹ If you think like a business owner, you will succeed. If you think only like a web designer, you will fail.

Taking Action Recap:

❶ Become a professional problem solver. Make this your number one priority.

❷ Have conversations that focus on problems and frustrations. Don't just guess; listening is essential.

❸ Start where your trust is highest. Use your current connections to start right away.

❹ Leverage your past results to get better projects. More past results = more future sales.

PARTING ADVICE

CHAPTER 9
Reinvest in Skills that Help You Create More Value

Don't get stuck as a freelancer forever.

I hope you are feeling inspired and motivated after reading through the Taking Action chapters. But before you go off to work towards achieving your dreams, I have a few last pieces of advice to help you find lifelong success.

My first piece of advice is simple: **as you are developing your freelancing career, make sure to continually reinvest in skills that help you create more value in the market**.

In other words, learn skills that will allow you to grow beyond just being a web designer.

As you begin to find success in your web design business and increase your income, it is essential to your long-term success to reinvest some of your earnings into your education. Increasing your knowledge base makes you more versatile and dynamic, as long as you invest in the right skills.

The skills we are referring to are general business and marketing skills, NOT skills related to design, coding, and other technical aspects.

While you already know that you must have an understanding of at least some web design-related skills to be an effective web designer, they are still only technical skills. To be the most successful you can be, you instead need to focus on building business skills.

You need to build business skills because first, technical skills don't help you land clients—they are only useful for completing the work you already have, and second, technical skills aren't easily transferable to areas outside of web design. It is unlikely that you will do web design forever, and when you decide to move to the next level, you will need a selection of other business skills already incorporated into your knowledge.

Since freelancing is a short-term goal, you do not want to limit yourself to only learning web design skills.

Instead, focus on learning skills like these:

- Sales
- Copywriting
- Communicating
- Effective self-management
- Negotiating
- Developing sales funnels
- Email marketing
- Market analysis

In other words, focus on investing in skills that make you a business problem-solver, not just a typical web designer who doesn't know much beyond coding. If you are unsure of which skill to learn first, becoming better at sales is always an ideal place to start.

If we think back to the tale of our two web designers, we can see how Ricky invested in different skills and received completely different results than Dave, who did not invest in learning other skills.

As Dave struggled to get new clients, let alone high-paying clients, he initially thought the price was the main factor. He eventually began to realize, though, that it was his lack of problem-solving skills. He knew the technical skills in theory, but he did not know how to use them to help other businesses.

Thanks to the question posed by his wife, Ricky invested his extra time and income into becoming a better problem solver. He improved his sales skills by focusing on the needs of his clients. Along with sales, he also worked on other skills, like copywriting, marketing and developing business systems. In a short time, Ricky became very skilled at helping solve all sorts of problems for many different types of businesses.

Eventually, Ricky realized that, since he had helped so many other businesses to grow and improve, he was more than capable of doing the same for himself. With the cash flow from his web design business as a security, all he needed was a good opportunity—which he spotted while working on a client's project. He was then able to use his experience, skills, and insight to begin creating his own business—confident in his ability to make it work.

Ricky found massive success, while Dave had to take a step back. Dave failed because he had built his career on a very narrow set of skills. He didn't have the wide skillset to solve problems or the ability to spot new opportunities, like Ricky. Since he saw his job as just code and design, he was not keeping an eye out for gaps in the market where he could create his own business. Many great opportunities passed him by because he did not build the knowledge or experience to notice them.

Keep these lessons in mind on your own journey. Technical skills only make you suitable to be an employee or freelancer, but business skills make you far more likely to be a business owner or entrepreneur. To make sure you win long-term, develop your business and sales skills.

◆◆◆

Parting Advice Recap:

❶ Reinvest in skills that help you create more value.

CHAPTER 10
KEEP THE END GOAL IN MIND

The end goal is long-term success and freedom.

I hope it's clear by now that the end goal is not to be the best web designer—it's to become the type of person who is ready to succeed in business long-term.

And this brings me to my second piece of parting advice: **always keep the end goal in mind.** Remember, freelancing is a way forward.

Earlier in the book, I mentioned that it is helpful to think of freelancing as a paid education. You should use what you have learned and the skills you have gained during your time as a freelancer to move on to something even better.

If you just focus on being a freelancer, there is often no light at the end of the tunnel. It is easy to get lost, feel burned out, or lose hope. Even if you are getting paid well, it can be hard to stay motivated and move forward.

If instead, you look at freelancing as an opportunity to get paid to learn business skills, things look very different. Now every sales call, client meeting, and project is an opportunity to learn. Even bad clients or projects will be useful as you are building the reference points and experience needed for when you branch out of web design to your next business venture.

Take a look back at our 3-Step Success Logic from the beginning of the book:

1. The best way to reach long-term success is as a business owner.
2. The way to become a successful business owner is by first learning to solve problems and provide value.

3. One of the best places to learn about business is through web design.

Our successful web designer, Ricky, never viewed web design as the end goal. He wanted to live life according to his terms and build a better life. His ultimate goal was freedom.

He realized early on that *thinking* like a business owner was the best way to sell his services. In the process, he *became* a business owner. As his business grew, he was making a good profit, but he still realized he would never achieve true freedom by only trading time for money.

This realization is what led to Ricky transitioning out of web design by hiring a small team to run and manage his web design business. Ricky used his web design time wisely and learned everything he needed to move on to the next stage of his business journey.

He was now ready to launch his own business and put all his new skills and experience into action. Using the marketing, sales, and business skills he had learned through web design, he was able to quickly grow and develop his new business idea.

Ricky was able to make his dreams and goals a reality because he had a real foundation of skills and experience to make it possible. While many people jump right into their big idea with no concrete plans for how to make it succeed, Ricky took a practical approach, which helped him make big gains each year.

Ricky, of course, is just an example made up for this book, but when you start looking, you will see real examples everywhere. MJ DeMarco, whom we mentioned earlier, used his time as a web design freelancer to help create his bigger business success and wealth.

All successful business owners started by using whatever opportunities they already had and then leveraging them as much as possible. With web design, this is the same approach you should be using. Look at web design as a way to get to the next level, rather than treating it as a never-ending freelancing gig.

While there is nothing wrong with freelancing in the beginning, make sure to keep the end goal in mind. Freelancing can be the best next step for you if it is part of a bigger plan. You must be able to connect the dots between the time you spend with web design freelancing and achieving your bigger goals later.

To wrap up this chapter, I want to tell you something I always tell my students: *the best web designers no longer work as web designers.*

What this means is that if you can succeed with web design—and I am sure you can—there are so many other industries out there where you can add a lot of value and countless other problems that you can solve.

When you become a web designer who can solve problems, this naturally leads to you moving on to other areas to build even bigger and better businesses. It is the natural progression of a web designer who thinks of web design in the right way.

So always keep your end goal in mind and focus on the skills and experience needed to get you there.

Parting Advice Recap:

❶ Reinvest in skills that help you create more value.
❷ Keep the end goal in mind.

CHAPTER 11
DON'T DELAY

Start small and start NOW.

No matter what your current situation is, there is no reason to put off taking that first step towards implementing what you have learned in this book so far. When you delay getting started, you delay being successful.

There are many reasons that people do not start right away. Some have already tried freelancing but got discouraged and quit when it didn't take off. Others feel stuck because they do not know which step to take next and are prisoners of "analysis paralysis." I don't want this to happen to you.

Whatever your current situation, there is no reason that you can't start taking action right away. The trick is to start small, start now, and just get going.

Now, I know this may feel intimidating. You might feel like you need the perfect idea or plan. A lot of people think they should have it all mapped out before they start, but it never works that way. The truth is the people who do succeed started with a less-than-perfect plan and found a way to make it work.

If you wait for all the lights to turn green before you start your car, you will never drive anywhere. It is just impossible to see the full path ahead and to know every step ahead. All you can do is pick the best direction possible for you right now and get going today.

When it comes to web design, avoid aiming for the $20,000 project right away. People often use this as a way to avoid failure - aiming for clients so big that it was never possible.

Also avoid spending another six months learning code online before you get started. You only need coding basics to get started, and you can learn these within a few days online.

Decide to commit and then start taking action now. Find a business and offer to help them solve a problem. By just making one website that solves a business problem, you are off to a great start. While this might seem like a very small step (and it is), it is the start of a much bigger journey. You need to first focus on taking action and building momentum because the big wins and profits will come later. The sooner you start the sooner they will arrive.

If you have read this book, then you have what you need to start now. You will still feel some doubt and possibly fear, but just start small, and the confidence and momentum will soon come. Trust yourself to make it work and take it step by step for now.

If I can do it, with zero web design experience and a ton of business failures behind me, then I know you can too. Believe in yourself and get going!

Parting Advice Recap:

❶ Reinvest in skills that help you create more value.
❷ Keep the end goal in mind.
❸ Start small and start NOW.

CHAPTER 12
You're Not Alone

Resources to help you achieve success.

As you've seen throughout these chapters, a major key to long-term success is *first* shifting your mindset and *then* taking the necessary steps to achieve your goals. You can have all the technical and coding skills in the world, but you can't achieve wealth and true freedom without first developing the right business mindset and taking the right steps.

This mindset can be a big jump for a lot of people who are new to business or have only focused on learning technical skills. Concepts like "value" and "problem-solving" might seem confusing or too abstract.

If you are feeling a little lost, don't worry. You don't have to go on this journey alone.

In the past, I also struggled. A lot. I was at a point where I thought I was the failure. I thought I was incapable of succeeding in business, and I felt like there was something wrong with me.

Looking back now, I see it was just my mindset and approach. It wasn't me that was the issue. It was just that I had never been taught how business really worked. I had only learned to think and act like an employee. I was still a capable person—I was just using a strategy that was never going to be successful.

But when I changed my mindset and my business approach, the results came fast. I was able to attract big clients, sell big deals, and make great profits. By thinking like a business owner and using the right approach to web design, I could finally feel myself making progress and succeeding in business. I started developing real skills that allowed me to build other businesses on top of web design and keep advancing.

A lot of people aren't this lucky, though. They don't figure out these mindset shifts in the early stages, so they end up failing or quitting.

They don't realize that they had all the skills and ability they needed, but they were only missing the right plan of action or the right mindset to make their success possible.

ACCELERATE YOUR PROGRESS WITH THE HELP OF OTHERS

By now, you know that you need to operate in the Mindset shifts that we covered in chapters 1–4.

- You know that results sell, not websites. A website is only ever a tool.
- You realize that business owners always care most about their core business needs; not design, coding or technical aspects.
- You're aware that the market pays you for the value you create; not your time, effort, background, or education.
- And you know that if you think like a business owner, you will be successful. If you think only like a web designer, you will fail.

You also know that you need to take the Action steps that we covered in chapters 5–8.

- You want to become a professional problem solver, and you're committed to making this your number one priority.
- You're planning to have conversations that focus on problems and frustrations.
- You will start where your trust is highest and use your current connections to start right away.

- And you intend to continually leverage your past results to get better projects.

Now, you're starting to put it all together with the parting advice we covered in chapters 9–11.

- You're committed to reinvest in skills that help you create more value.
- You know to always keep the end goal in mind.
- You will start small and start NOW.

But the piece that really cements your likelihood of success is when you have the *help and support of others*.

Every web designer runs into obstacles and problems to solve. But if you're all alone on your journey, you have to solve them all by yourself. It can be lonely, confusing, and time-consuming to figure out your own solutions to every problem.

You know you have potential within yourself. But when you're alone, it's easy to feel paralyzed by all the practical questions that arise.

"How do I raise my rates?"

"Why aren't people hiring me?"

"How do I find the good clients? And when I find them, how do I reach out to them?"

"Am I good enough to sell my work?"

"How do I get better at solving big problems?"

Something as small as a script for a cold email can leave you frozen and stuck for days or weeks while you're wondering, "What do I say?"

Imagine what a difference it would make if you could just reach out to someone in that moment and get a script that you can adapt to your needs.

When you're alone, there's also the danger that you could get frustrated and give up. Think about Dave. From our third-party viewpoint, it's easy to see that he needed to change his mindset and his actions. But when you're in Dave's shoes, it's not so easy to see that about yourself.

Just imagine if Dave could talk to Ricky and say, "Hey man, what am I doing wrong? You just started and you're crushing it. I've been working in this field for years and I can't make any progress. Can you share what's working or what I might be missing?"

WHEN YOU HAVE THE SUPPORT OF OTHERS WHO ARE ON THE SAME JOURNEY, IT CHANGES EVERYTHING.

When you follow in the footsteps of others who are just ahead of you, you can quickly see how they solved the same problems. You can take advantage of their solutions to move forward. And you can stay motivated and inspired as you see what's possible just one step ahead of you.

But where and how do you find people who will help you?

It's not always easy.

Some people might view you as a potential competitor, so they keep their cards close to their chest and won't share what's working.

Other people might be trapped in a mindset more like Dave's. Even though they have knowledge and skills, their business isn't working that well for them. They themselves are stuck, so they're not much help.

Other people might just be indifferent. They don't really care if they're not lending a hand to those who are coming behind them.

But finding a supportive environment shouldn't come down to luck or random chance.

This is why I started Fox Web School.

FOX WEB SCHOOL WAS CREATED FOR ASPIRING ENTREPRENEURS AND FREELANCERS LIKE YOU WHO WANT TO BE SUCCESSFUL.

If you're embarking on your journey as a web designer, and you want to be surrounded by a community of helpful, supportive people who "get it," Fox Web School was created just for you.

At Fox Web School, you will receive the best advice to set you on the right path. I created this community to show aspiring web designers what works and how to focus on the foundational business mindset and skills needed to win.

It's a place where you can get support, training, and practical help for running a successful web design business.

It's a safe environment where you can change your mindset, take action, and get better at thinking like a business owner. It is also a place where you can get practical advice on how to reach out to prospective clients, win their trust, and close the sale.

There are two levels of how you can take advantage of Fox Web School.

Free Resources:

When I first started web design, I did not have much savings or an income, so I know how that feels. If you are in the same situation, we have a few resources to help you get going.

- Watch the free Fox Web School YouTube channel:
  https://www.youtube.com/foxwebschool
- Join our email list for more free resources:
  https://foxwebschool.com/newsletter
- Also, this book comes with a series of emails to help you put what you've just learned into action; sign up here:
  https://foxwebschool.com/extrahelp

Coaching Program:

If you do have extra resources and are willing to commit to making the most progress possible, we offer a private coaching program available within the school.

Fox Web School is the only online web design school that focuses on *more* than just code. We teach aspiring entrepreneurs and freelancers like yourself the full set of business skills and mindsets that will enable our students to sell web design services and get great results for their clients, so that they can go on to accomplish even bigger dreams.

In other words, our core focus is on getting results that matter.

Inside the Fox Sales Legends, our private coaching program, you'll get group coaching and support, accountability systems, video training, group and guest live calls, effective sales templates and scripts, plus much more.

About Fox Sales Legends

Our group coaching program is anything but average. We start by teaching you what you need to know about web design to be a successful freelancer, but we also see the big picture.

We teach you what you need to know to move forward as a successful business owner—whether it be in web design or something else entirely. We also provide you with a supportive community of web designers who are working towards growth, just like you.

- In the short term (right away), you'll want to learn how to land your first few projects.
- In the medium term (2-3 years), you'll want to stabilize your income, build a solid base of clients and referrals, help businesses in a big way, and start to be seen as more of a trusted advisor than a freelancer.
- In the long term (3-5 years), our end goal is much bigger than just helping you make some websites. This last stage is really what separates our school from other courses. As much as we love web design (and we do!), **we always see it more of a launching pad than an end destination**. Our end goal is always for our students to use their web design experience to go on to even <u>bigger and better things</u> (like Ricky did).

At Fox Web School, we have a long-term success mindset. We realize that you may not want to do web design forever. Maybe you want to create a massive business empire or just build several consistent sources of income that can fund your dream lifestyle. Whatever your ideal vision for your life, we want to give you the skills and know-how to make it possible. Fox Web School is a web design school for people who are thinking bigger than just freelancing.

If you are looking at freelancing as a means to a bigger end, because you need the resources and flexibility from your freelance work to eventually pursue the REAL thing you care about, then you're in the right place.

Fox Web School's Core Values

At Fox Web School, our values are very important to us and help us make decisions about how to best educate our students.

When you learn at Fox Web School, you can always expect the following values to be reflected in our teaching style.

Honesty and Integrity

We care about providing high value. We create products that we believe in and that we feel good about selling. Our students can expect to have a valuable experience when they learn from us.

We don't make empty promises or offer things we can't fulfil. We want to make good money, but we want to keep a clear conscience, knowing that all our students receive great value.

No Hype

We hate spam, hype, and annoying self-promotion. We reject the "overnight success" mindset. We don't use shady marketing trends or fill your head with empty promises. We see ourselves as trusted business partners, not out-of-reach gurus on a mountain.

A Community that Matters

A community that helps students accomplish their goals is one of the most important parts of our business. People want to be around people who think positively and take action.

When our students want to learn web design, we know that what they really want is freedom and autonomy. They see web design as a stepping stone to get to their goals. Hopefully, after reading this book, you have adopted this mindset.

FIND OUT MORE ABOUT FOX SALES LEGENDS

If you are willing to commit to making the most progress possible, surrounded by a supportive community of web designers who share a long-term success mindset and who are working towards growth, just like you, send us an application! Here's where you can find out all the details and apply.

To learn about the Fox Sales Legends coaching program, with student reviews, program details and pricing, just go here: **https://foxwebschool.com /foxsaleslegends/**

Wrapping it all up

Now that you've reached the end of this book, you've hopefully realized that anyone can learn the practical principles that helped make Ricky successful, and you know how to avoid the mistakes that Dave made.

Now it's time to go beyond feeling inspired. It's your turn. So go out and take advantage of the mindset shifts and the action steps that we've discussed. And if you want the support of other people, you know that Fox Web School has your back!

Welcome to your new territory as a successful, high-paid web designer. Go forth and conquer!

I wish you the best of luck on your journey to success. Fox Web School is always here if you need a helping hand.

Also, don't be a stranger! I'd love to interact with you in the YouTube comment section on the Fox Web School's channel or on the Fastlane Forum. Drop me a line!

THANK YOU!

A large part of anyone's success is going to be based on who they surround them-selves with and I am no different. I would like to quickly thank several people who made all of this possible.

Alex Dubis

Alex Dubis is my business partner, and has helped in a big way to build the school to where it currently is. She works a lot behind the scenes, but does so much to help the students and the Fox community. Thanks Alex for everything. You're a star!

The Fastlane Forums

MJ DeMarco and the gang over on the Fastlane forums have done so much to help me on my journey. If there is one online forum/resource I recommend everyone to check out, it is the Fastlane Forum and the books of MJ DeMarco.

The Fox Students

Although it sounds a little cheesy to write it in this book, these are such a great group of people. It's been a pleasure to work alongside all of you. A lot of you took a big risk joining, and it has been so cool to be a part of your journey and try help as much as I could. Thanks everyone!

My Wolfpack Mastermind Group

These are some great guys I have had the luck of working together with over the last year, and it has been amazing. Dan, Chuck, Game, Wouter, Bradley and Jordan - massive thanks, and I know you are all going to crush it with your own projects and personal success.

My Family

Mum, Dad, Paul, Gearoid, Melinda and Dave - thank you for all the support.

Book Help

A massive thanks to Martin for his help with this ebook, and making it possible for this to even exist. What started as a 10 page guide quickly grew, and you stuck with it till the end! Thank you.

... and finally to you, the Reader

I really hope this book helps in a big way, and thank you for your support! I wish you all the best, and hope you get what you are after.